INTRODU

INTRODUCING TYNDALE

An Extract from Tyndale's

An Answer to Sir Thomas More's Dialogue

With an Introduction by John Piper and
an Epilogue by Robert J. Sheehan

THE BANNER OF TRUTH TRUST

THE BANNER OF TRUTH TRUST

3 Murrayfield Road, Edinburgh EH12 6EL, UK
PO Box 621, Carlisle, PA 17013, USA

*

This selection © The Banner of Truth Trust 2017

Introduction from *Filling Up the Afflictions of Christ* by
John Piper, © 2009. Used by permission of Crossway,
a publishing ministry of Good News Publishers,
Wheaton, IL 60187, USA, www.crossway.org.

Epilogue used by permission of Mrs Wendy Evers.

*

ISBN
Print: 978 1 84871 755 8
EPUB: 978 1 84871 756 5
Kindle: 978 1 84871 757 2

*

Typeset in 11/15 pt Adobe Garamond Pro at
The Banner of Truth Trust, Edinburgh
Printed in the USA by
Versa Press, Inc.,
East Peoria, IL.

Contents

INTRODUCTION

'Always Singing One Note'—
A Vernacular Bible

Why William Tyndale Lived and Died

John Piper

What was the 'one note' he always sang?

Stephen Vaughan was an English merchant commissioned by Thomas Cromwell, the king's adviser, to find William Tyndale and inform him that King Henry VIII desired him to come back to England out of hiding on the continent. In a letter to Cromwell from Vaughan dated June 19, 1531, Vaughan wrote about Tyndale (1494–1536) these simple words: 'I find him always singing one note.'[1] That one note was this: Will the King of England give his official endorsement to a vernacular Bible for all his English subjects? If not, Tyndale will

---

[1] David Daniell, *William Tyndale: A Biography* (New Haven: Yale University Press, 1994), p. 217.

not come. If so, Tyndale will give himself up to the king and never write another book.

This was the driving passion of his life—to see the Bible translated from the Greek and Hebrew into ordinary English available for every person in England to read.

Whatever it costs

Henry VIII was angry with Tyndale for believing and promoting Martin Luther's Reformation teachings. In particular he was angry because of Tyndale's book, *Answer to Sir Thomas More*. Thomas More (famous for his book *Utopia*, and the subject of the 1966 British movie *A Man for All Seasons*) was the Lord Chancellor who helped Henry VIII write his repudiation of Luther called *Defence of the Seven Sacraments*. Thomas More was thoroughly Roman Catholic and radically anti-Reformation, anti-Luther, and anti-Tyndale. So Tyndale had come under the same excoriating criticism by Thomas More.[2] In fact More had a 'near-rabid hatred'[3] for Tyndale and published three long responses to him totalling near three-quarters of a million words.[4]

But in spite of this high court anger against Tyndale, the king's message to Tyndale, carried by Vaughan, was mercy:

[2] For example, in More's 1529 book, *Dialogue Concerning Heresies*.

[3] Daniell, *Tyndale*, p. 4.

[4] Thomas More wrote vastly more to condemn Tyndale than Tyndale wrote in his defence. After one book called *An Answer Unto Sir Thomas More's Dialogue* (1531), Tyndale was done. For Thomas More, however, there were 'close on three quarters of a million words against Tyndale … [compared to] Tyndale's eighty thousand in his *Answer*'. *Ibid.*, p. 277.

'The kings' royal majesty is ... inclined to mercy, pity, and compassion.'[5]

The thirty-seven-year-old Tyndale was moved to tears by this offer of mercy. He had been an exile from his homeland for seven years. But then he sounds his 'one note' again: Will the king authorize a vernacular English Bible from the original languages? Vaughan gives us Tyndale's words from May, 1531:

> I assure you, if it would stand with the King's most gracious pleasure to grant only a bare text of the Scripture [that is, without explanatory notes] to be put forth among his people, like as is put forth among the subjects of the emperor in these parts, and of other Christian princes, be it of the translation of what person soever shall please his Majesty, I shall immediately make faithful promise never to write more, nor abide two days in these parts after the same: but immediately to repair unto his realm, and there most humbly submit myself at the feet of his royal majesty, offering my body to suffer what pain or torture, yea, what death his grace will, so this [translation] be obtained. Until that time, I will abide the asperity of all chances, whatsoever shall come, and endure my life in as many pains as it is able to bear and suffer.[6]

In other words, Tyndale will give himself up to the king on one condition—that the king authorize an English Bible translated from the Greek and Hebrew into the common language of the people.

[5] *Ibid.*, p. 216.
[6] *Ibid.*

The king refused. And Tyndale never went to his homeland again. Instead, if the king and the Roman Catholic Church would not provide a printed Bible in English for the common man to read, Tyndale would, even if it cost him his life—which it did five years later.

As I live, the plowboy will know his Bible

When he was twenty-eight years old in 1522, he was serving as a tutor in the home of John Walsh in Gloucestershire spending most of his time studying Erasmus' Greek New Testament which had been printed six years before in 1516. And we should pause here and make clear what an incendiary thing this Greek New Testament was in history. David Daniell describes the magnitude of this event:

> This was the first time that the Greek New Testament had been printed. It is no exaggeration to say that it set fire to Europe. Luther [1483-1546] translated it into his famous German version of 1522. In a few years there appeared translations from the Greek into most European vernaculars. They were the true basis of the popular reformation.[7]

[7] William Tyndale, *Selected Writings,* edited with an introduction by David Daniell (New York: Routledge, 2003), p. ix. 'Modern champions of the Catholic position like to support a view of the Reformation, that it was entirely a political imposition by a ruthless minority in power against both the traditions and the wishes of the pious people of England. ... The energy which affected every human life in northern Europe, however, came from a different place. It was not the result of political imposition. It came from the discovery of the Word of God as originally written ... in the language of the people. Moreover, it could be read and understood, without censorship by the Church or mediation through the Church. ... Such reading produced a totally different view of everyday Christianity: the weekly, daily, even

Every day William Tyndale was seeing the Reformation truths more clearly in the Greek New Testament as an ordained Catholic priest. Increasingly he was making himself suspect in this Catholic house of John Walsh. Learned men would come for dinner, and Tyndale would discuss the things he was seeing in the New Testament. John Foxe tells us that one day an exasperated Catholic scholar at dinner with Tyndale said, 'We were better be without God's law than the pope's.'

In response Tyndale spoke his famous words, 'I defy the Pope and all his laws. … If God spare my life ere many years, I will cause a boy that driveth the plow, shall know more of the Scripture than thou dost.'[8]

The one-note crescendo

Four years later Tyndale finished the English translation of the Greek New Testament in Worms, Germany, and began to smuggle it into England in bales of cloth. He had grown up in Gloucestershire, the cloth-working county, and now we see what that turn of providence was about.[9] By October

---

hourly ceremonies so lovingly catalogued by some Catholic revisionists are not there; purgatory is not there; there is no aural confession and penance. Two supports of the Church's wealth and power collapsed. Instead there was simply individual faith in Christ the Saviour, found in Scripture. That and only that "justified" the sinner, whose root failings were now in the face of God, not the bishops or the pope.' Daniell, *Tyndale*, p. 58.

[8] Daniell, *Tyndale*, p. 79.

[9] 'Not for nothing did William Tyndale, exiled in Cologne, Worms and Antwerp, use the international trade routes of the cloth merchants to get his books into England, smuggled in bales of cloth.' *Ibid.*, p. 15.

of 1526 the book had been banned by Bishop Tunstall in London, but the print run was at least three thousand. And the books were getting to the people. Over the next eight years, five pirated editions were printed as well.[10]

In 1534 Tyndale published a revised New Testament, having learned Hebrew in the meantime, probably in Germany, which helped him better understand the connections between the Old and New Testaments. Daniell calls this 1534 New Testament 'the glory of his life's work'.[11] If Tyndale was 'always singing one note', this was the crescendo of the song of his life—the finished and refined New Testament in English.

The very first New Testament in English from the Greek

For the first time ever in history, the Greek New Testament was translated into English. And for the first time ever the New Testament in English was available in a printed form. Before Tyndale there were only hand-written manuscripts of the Bible in English. These manuscripts we owe to the work and inspiration of John Wycliffe and the Lollards[12] from 130 years earlier.[13] For a thousand years the only translation of the Greek and Hebrew Bible was the Latin Vulgate, and few people could understand it, even if they had access to it.

[10] *Ibid.*, p. 188.

[11] *Ibid.*, p. 316.

[12] 'In the summer of 1382, Wycliffe was attacked in a sermon preached at St. Mary's, Oxford, and his followers were for the first time denounced as "Lollards"—a loose and suitably meaningless term of abuse ("mutterers") current in the Low Countries for Bible students, and thus heretics.' David Daniell, *The Bible in English: Its History and Influence* (New Haven: Yale University Press, 2003), p. 73.

[13] Gutenberg's printing press came in 1450.

Before he was martyred in 1536 Tyndale had translated into clear, common English[14] not only the New Testament[15] but also the Pentateuch, Joshua to 2 Chronicles, and Jonah.[16] All this material became the basis of the *Great Bible* issued by Miles Coverdale in England in 1539[17] and of the *Geneva Bible* published in 1560—'the Bible of the nation',[18] which sold over a million copies between 1560 and 1640.

Under God, Tyndale gave us our English Bible

We do not get a clear sense of Tyndale's achievement without some comparisons. We think of the dominant King James Version as giving us the pervasive language of the English Bible. But Daniell clarifies the situation:

[14] 'Tyndale transmitted an English strength which is the opposite of Latin, seen in the difference between "high" and "elevated", "gift" and "donation", "many" and "multitudinous".' Daniell, *Tyndale*, p. 3.

[15] Tyndale did not follow Luther in putting Hebrews, James, Jude, and Revelation in a special section of the New Testament set apart as inferior. 'Tyndale, as shown later by his preface to James in his 1534 New Testament, is not only wiser and more generous—he is more true to the New Testament.' *Ibid.*, p. 120.

[16] This is available now in print with all its original notes and introductions: *Tyndale's Old Testament, translated by William Tyndale* (New Haven: Yale University Press, 1992); as is *Tyndale's New Testament, translated by William Tyndale* (New Haven: Yale University Press, 1989).

[17] How could it be that Tyndale was martyred in 1536 for translating the Bible into English, and that his New Testament could be burned in London by Bishop Tunstall, and yet an entire printed Bible, essentially Tyndale's, *The Great Bible*, could be published in England three years later officially endorsed by this Bible-burning bishop? Daniell explains: 'Tunstall, whose name would shortly appear on the title pages approving two editions of the Great Bible, was playing politics, being a puppet of the Pope through Wolsey and the king, betraying his Christian humanist learning at the direction of the church, needing to be receiving [Thomas] Wolsey's favour. ... To burn God's word for politics was to Tyndale barbarous.' *Tyndale*, p. 93.

[18] Tyndale, *Selected Writings*, p. xi.

William Tyndale gave us our English Bible. The sages assembled by King James to prepare the Authorised Version of 1611, so often praised for unlikely corporate inspiration, took over Tyndale's work. Nine-tenths of the Authorised Version's New Testament is Tyndale's. The same is true of the first half of the Old Testament, which was as far as he was able to get before he was executed outside Brussels in 1536.[19]

Here is a sampling of the English phrases we owe to Tyndale:

'Let there be light' (Gen. 1:3).

'Am I my brother's keeper?' (Gen. 4:9).

'The Lord bless thee and keep thee. The Lord make his face to shine upon thee and be merciful unto thee. The Lord lift up his countenance upon thee, and give thee peace' (Num. 6:24-26).

'In the beginning was the Word and the Word was with God and the Word was God' (John 1:1).

---

[19] *Tyndale*, p. 1. Daniell speaks with more precision elsewhere and says that the Authorised Version is 83 per cent Tyndale's (Tyndale, *Selected Writings*, p. vii). Brian Moynahan, in *God's Bestseller: William Tyndale, Thomas More, and the Writing of the English Bible—A Story of Martyrdom and Betrayal* (New York: St Martin's Press, 2002, p. 1), confirms this with his estimates: Tyndale's words 'account for 84 percent of the [King James Version] New Testament and 75.8 percent of the Old Testament books that he translated'. Daniell also points out how remarkable the Old Testament translations were: 'These opening chapters of Genesis are the first translations—not just the first printed, but the first translations—from Hebrew into English. This needs to be emphasized. Not only was the Hebrew language only known in England in 1529 and 1530 by, at the most, a tiny handful of scholars in Oxford and Cambridge, and quite possibly by none; that there was a language called Hebrew at all, or that it had any connection whatsoever with the Bible, would have been news to most of the ordinary population.' *Tyndale*, p. 287.

'There were shepherds abiding in the field' (Luke 2:8).

'Blessed are they that mourn for they shall be comforted' (Matt. 5:4).

'Our Father, which art in heaven, hallowed be thy name' (Matt. 6:9).

'The signs of the times' (Matt. 16:3).

'The spirit is willing but the flesh is weak' (Matt. 26:41).

'He went out … and wept bitterly' (Matt. 26:75). Those two words 'wept bitterly' are still used by almost all modern translations (NIV, NASB, ESV, NKJV). The expression has not been improved on for five hundred years in spite of weak efforts like one recent translation: 'cried hard'. Unlike that phrase, 'the rhythm of his two words carries the experience'.[20]

'A law unto themselves' (Rom. 2:14).

'In him we live, move and have our being' (Acts 17:28).

'Though I speak with the tongues of men and of angels' (1 Cor. 13:1).

'Fight the good fight' (1 Tim. 6:12).

According to Daniell, 'The list of such near-proverbial phrases is endless.'[21] Five hundred years after his great work 'newspaper headlines still quote Tyndale, though unknowingly, and he has reached more people than even Shakespeare'.[22]

---

[20] Tyndale, *Selected Writings*, p. xv.
[21] Daniell, *Tyndale*, p. 142.
[22] *Ibid.*, p. 2.

He gave us new prose—and a reformation

Luther's translation of 1522 is often praised for 'having given a language to the emerging German nation'. Daniell claims the same for Tyndale in English:

> In his Bible translations, Tyndale's conscious use of everyday words, without inversions, in a neutral word-order, and his wonderful ear for rhythmic patterns, gave to English not only a Bible language, but a new prose. England was blessed as a nation in that the language of its principal book, as the Bible in English rapidly became, was the fountain from which flowed the lucidity, suppleness and expressive range of the greatest prose thereafter.[23]

His craftsmanship with the English language amounted to genius.[24] He translated two-thirds of the Bible so well that his translations have endured until today.[25]

This was not merely a literary phenomenon; it was a spiritual explosion. Tyndale's Bible and writings were the kindling that set the Reformation on fire in England.

Two ways to die to bear fruit for God

The question arises: How did William Tyndale accomplish this historic achievement? We can answer this in Tyndale's

[23] *Ibid.*, p. 116.

[24] Tyndale, *Selected Writings*, p. xv.

[25] Daniell, *Tyndale*, p. 121. 'Tyndale gave the nation a Bible language that was English in words, word-order and lilt. He invented some words (for example, "scapegoat") and the great Oxford English Dictionary has mis-attributed, and thus also mis-dated, a number of his first uses.' (*Ibid.*, p. 3.)

case by remembering two ways that a pastor must die in the ministry. We must die to the notion that we do not have to think hard or work hard to achieve spiritual goals. And we must die to the notion that our thinking and our working is decisive in achieving spiritual goals.

Paul said in 2 Timothy 2:7, 'Think over what I say, for the Lord will give you understanding in everything.' First, think. Work. Don't bypass the hard work of thinking about apostolic truth. But second, remember this: 'The Lord will give you understanding.' You work. He gives. If he withholds, all our working is in vain. But he ordains that we use our minds and that we work in achieving spiritual ends. So Paul says in 1 Corinthians 15:10, 'I worked harder than any of them, though it was not I, but the grace of God that is with me.' The key to spiritual achievement is to work hard, and to know and believe and feel and be happy that God's sovereign grace is the decisive cause of all the good that comes.

How Erasmus and Tyndale were alike

The way these two truths come together in Tyndale's life explains how he could accomplish what he did. And one of the best ways to see it is to compare him with Erasmus, the Roman Catholic humanist scholar who was famous for his books *Enchiridion* and *The Praise of Folly* and for his printed Greek New Testament.

Erasmus was twenty-eight years older than Tyndale, but they both died in 1536—Tyndale martyred by the Roman

Catholic Church, Erasmus a respected member of that church. Erasmus had spent time in Oxford and Cambridge, but we don't know if he and Tyndale ever met.

On the surface, one sees remarkable similarities between Tyndale and Erasmus. Both were great linguists. Erasmus was a Latin scholar and produced the first printed Greek New Testament. Tyndale knew eight languages: Latin, Greek, German, French, Hebrew, Spanish, Italian, and English. Both men loved the natural power of language and were part of a rebirth of interest in the way language works.

For example, Erasmus wrote a book called *De copia* that Tyndale no doubt used as a student at Oxford.[26] It helped students increase their abilities to exploit the 'copious' potential of language. This was hugely influential in the early 1500s in England and was used to train students in the infinite possibilities of varied verbal expression. The aim was to keep that language from sinking down to mere jargon and worn-out slang and uncreative, unimaginative, prosaic, colourless, boring speech.

One practice lesson for students from *De copia* was to give 'no fewer than one hundred and fifty ways of saying "Your letter has delighted me very much"'. The point was to force students 'to use of all the verbal muscles in order to avoid any hint of flabbiness'.[27] It is not surprising that this is the kind of educational world that gave rise to William Shakespeare

[26] 'Tyndale could hardly have missed *De copia*.' Daniell, *Tyndale*, p. 43. This book went through 150 editions by 1572.

[27] *Ibid.*, p. 42.

(who was born in 1564). Shakespeare is renowned for his unparalleled use of copiousness in language. One critic wrote, 'Without Erasmus, no Shakespeare.'[28]

So both Erasmus and Tyndale were educated in an atmosphere of conscious craftsmanship.[29] That is, they both believed in hard work to say things clearly and creatively and compellingly when they spoke for Christ.

Not only that, but they both believed the Bible should be translated into the vernacular of every language. Erasmus wrote in the preface to his Greek New Testament,

> Christ wishes his mysteries to be published as widely as possible. I would wish even all women to read the gospel and the epistles of St. Paul, and I wish that they were translated into all languages of all Christian people, that they might be read and known, not merely by the Scotch and the Irish, but even by the Turks and the Saracens. I wish that the husbandman may sing parts of them at his plow, that the weaver may warble them at his shuttle, that the traveller may with their narratives beguile the weariness of the way.[30]

Tyndale could not have said it better.

Both were concerned with the corruption and abuses in the Catholic Church, and both wrote about Christ and the

---

[28] Emrys Jones, *The Origins of Shakespeare* (New York: Oxford University Press, 1977), p. 13.

[29] 'Tyndale as conscious craftsman has been not just neglected, but denied: yet the evidence of the book that follows makes it beyond challenge that he used, as a master, the skill it she selection and arrangement of words which he partly learned at school and university, and partly developed from pioneering work by Erasmus.' Daniell, *Tyndale*, p. 2.

[30] *Ibid.*, p. 67.

Christian life. Tyndale even translated Erasmus' *Enchiridion*, a kind of spiritual handbook for the Christian life—what Erasmus called *philosophia Christi*.

From a lightning bug to a lightning bolt

But there was a massive difference between these men, and it had directly to do with the other half of the paradox, namely, that we must die not just to intellectual and linguistic laziness, but also to human presumption—human self-exaltation and self-sufficiency. Erasmus and Luther had clashed in the 1520s over the freedom of the will—Erasmus defending human self-determination and Luther arguing for the depravity and bondage of the will.[31] Tyndale was firmly with Luther here.

> Our will is locked and knit faster under the will of the devil than could an hundred thousand chains bind a man unto a post.[32]

> Because … [by] nature we are evil, therefore we both think and do evil, and are under vengeance under the law, convict to eternal damnation by the law, and are contrary to the will of God in all our will and in all things consent to the will of the fiend.[33]

> It is not possible for a natural man to consent to the law, that it should be good, or that God should be righteous which maketh the law.[34]

---

[31] Erasmus' book was titled *On the Freedom of the Will*, and Luther's was *The Bondage of the Will*.

[32] Tyndale, *Selected Writings*, p. 39.

[33] *Ibid.*, p. 37.

[34] *Ibid.*, p. 40.

This view of human sinfulness set the stage for Tyndale's grasp of the glory of God's sovereign grace in the gospel. Erasmus—and Thomas More with him—did not see the depth of the human condition, their own condition, and so did not see the glory and explosive power of what the reformers saw in the New Testament. What the reformers like Tyndale and Luther saw was not a *philosophia Christi* but the massive work of God in the death and resurrection of Christ to save hopelessly enslaved and hell-bound sinners.

Erasmus does not live or write in this realm of horrible condition and gracious blood-bought salvation. He has the appearance of reform in the *Enchiridion*, but something is missing. To walk from Erasmus into Tyndale is to move (to paraphrase Mark Twain) from a lightning bug to a lightning bolt.

Daniell puts it like this:

> Something in the *Enchiridion* is missing. … It is a masterpiece of humanist piety. … [But] the activity of Christ in the Gospels, his special work of salvation so strongly detailed there and in the epistles of Paul, is largely missing. Christologically, where Luther thunders, Erasmus makes a sweet sound: what to Tyndale was an impregnable stronghold feels in the *Enchiridion* like a summer pavilion.[35]

Where Luther and Tyndale were blood-earnest about our dreadful human condition and the glory of salvation in Christ, Erasmus and Thomas More joked and bantered.

[35] Daniell, *Tyndale*, pp. 68-69.

When Luther published his 95 theses in 1517, Erasmus sent a copy of them to More—along with a 'jocular letter including the anti-papal games, and witty satirical diatribes against abuses within the church, which both of them loved to make'.[36]

The difference: clarity and seriousness about the gospel

I linger here with this difference between Tyndale and Erasmus because I am trying to penetrate to how Tyndale accomplished what he did through translating the New Testament. Explosive reformation is what he accomplished in England. This was not the effect of Erasmus' highbrow, elitist, layered nuancing of Christ and church tradition. Erasmus and Thomas More may have satirized the monasteries and clerical abuses, but they were always playing games compared to Tyndale.

And in this they were very much like notable Christian writers in our own day. Listen to this remarkable assessment from Daniell, and see if you do not hear a description of certain writers in our day who belittle doctrine and extol ambiguity as the humble and mature mind-set:

> Not only is there no fully realized Christ or Devil in Erasmus's book …: there is a touch of irony about it all, with a feeling of the writer cultivating a faintly superior ambiguity: as if to be dogmatic, for example about the full theology of the work of Christ, was to be rather distasteful, below the best, elite, humanist heights. … By contrast Tyndale … is ferociously

[36] *Ibid.*, p. 254.

single-minded ['always singing one note']; the matter in hand, the immediate access of the soul to God without intermediary, is far too important for hints of faintly ironic superiority. … Tyndale is as four-square as a carpenter's tool. But in Erasmus's account of the origins of his book there is a touch of the sort of layering of ironies found in the games with *personae*.[37]

It is ironic and sad that today supposedly avant-garde Christian writers can strike this cool, evasive, imprecise, artistic, superficially reformist pose of Erasmus and call it '*post*-modern' and capture a generation of unwitting, historically naïve, emergent people who don't know they are being duped by the same old verbal tactics used by the elitist humanist writers in past generations. We can see them in Athanasius' day (the slippery Arians at Nicaea), and we see them now in Tyndale's day. It's not post-modern. It's pre-modern—because it is perpetual.

At root: a passion for justification by faith

What drove Tyndale to sing 'one note' all his life was the rock-solid conviction that all humans were in bondage to sin, blind, dead, damned, and helpless, and that God had acted in Christ to provide salvation by grace through faith. This is what lay hidden in the Latin Scriptures and the church system of penance and merit. The Bible must be translated for the sake of the liberating, life-giving gospel.[38]

---

[37] *Ibid.*, pp. 69-70.

[38] 'Central to Tyndale's insistence on the need for the Scriptures in English was his grasp that Paul had to be understood in relation to each reader's salvation, and he needed there, above all, to be clear.' *Ibid.*, p. 139.

There is only one hope for our liberation from the bonds of sin and eternal condemnation, Tyndale said: 'Neither can any creature loose the bonds, save the blood of Christ only.'[39]

> By grace ... we are plucked out of Adam the ground of all evil and graffed [*sic*] in Christ, the root of all goodness. In Christ God loved us, his elect and chosen, before the world began and reserved us unto the knowledge of his Son and of his holy gospel: and when the gospel[40] is preached to us openeth our hearts and giveth us grace to believe, and putteth the spirit of Christ in us: and we know him as our Father most merciful, and consent to the law and love it inwardly in our heart and desire to fulfil it and sorrow because we do not.[41]

This massive dose of bondage to sin and deliverance by blood-bought sovereign grace[42] is missing in Erasmus. This

[39] Tyndale, *Selected Writings*, p. 40.

[40] Here is Tyndale's definition of the 'gospel' that rings with exuberant joy: '*Evangelion* (that we call the gospel) is a Greek word and signifieth good, merry, glad and joyful tidings, that maketh a man's heart glad and maketh him sing, dance, and leap for joy. ... [This gospel is] all of Christ the right David, how that he hath fought with sin, with death, and the devil, and overcome them: whereby all men that were in bondage to sin, wounded with death, overcome of the devil are without their own merits or deservings loosed, justified, restored to life and saved, brought to liberty and reconciled unto the favor of God and set at one with him again: which tidings as many as believe laud, praise and thank God, are glad, sing and dance for joy.' *Ibid.*, p. 33.

[41] *Ibid.*, p. 37.

[42] 'Tyndale was more than a mildly theological thinker. He is at last being understood as, theologically as well as linguistically, well ahead of his time. For him, as several decades later for Calvin (and in the twentieth century Karl Barth), the overriding message of the New Testament is the sovereignty of God. Everything is contained in that. It must never, as he wrote, be lost from sight. ... Tyndale, we are now being shown, was original and new—except that he was also old, demonstrating the understanding of God as revealed in the whole New Testament. For Tyndale,

is why there is an elitist lightness to his religion—just like there is to so much of evangelicalism today. Hell and sin and atonement and sovereign grace were not weighty realities for him. But for Tyndale they were everything. And in the middle of these great realities was the doctrine of justification by faith alone. This is why the Bible had to be translated, and ultimately this is why Tyndale was martyred.

> By faith are we saved only in believing the promises. And though faith be never without love and good works, yet is our saving imputed neither to love nor unto good works but unto faith only.[43]

> Faith the mother of all good works justifieth us, before we can bring forth any good work: as the husband marryeth his wife before he can have any lawful children by her.[44]

This is the answer to how William Tyndale accomplished what he did in translating the New Testament and writing books that set England on fire with the reformed faith. He worked assiduously like the most skilled artist in the craft of compelling translation, and he was deeply passionate about the great doctrinal truths of the gospel of sovereign grace.

Man is lost, spiritually dead, condemned. God is sovereign; Christ is sufficient. Faith is all. Bible translation and Bible truth were inseparable for Tyndale, and in the end it was the

---

God is, above all, sovereign, active in the individual and in history. He is the one, as he put it, in whom alone is found salvation and flourishing.' *Ibid.*, pp. viii-ix.

[43] *Ibid.*, p. 38.

[44] Daniell, *Tyndale*, pp. 156-157.

truth—especially the truth of justification by faith—that ignited Britain with reformed fire and then brought the death sentence to this Bible translator.

Blood-serious opposition to Bible translation

It is almost incomprehensible to us how viciously opposed the Roman Catholic Church was to the translation of the Scriptures into English. John Wycliffe and his followers called 'Lollards'[45] had spread written manuscripts of English translations from the Latin in the late 1300s. In 1401 Parliament passed the law *de Haeretico Comburendo*—'on the burning of heretics'—to make heresy punishable by burning people alive at the stake. The Bible translators were in view.

Then in 1408 the Archbishop of Canterbury, Thomas Arundell, created the *Constitutions of Oxford*, which said,

> It is a dangerous thing, as witnesseth blessed St. Jerome, to translate the text of the Holy Scripture out of one tongue into another, for in the translation the same sense is not always easily kept. … We therefore decree and ordain, that no man, hereafter, by his own authority translate any text of the Scripture into English or any other tongue … and that no man can read any such book … in part or in whole.[46]

Together these statutes meant that you could be burned alive by the Catholic Church for simply reading the Bible in English. The dramatist John Bale (1495–1563) 'as a boy of 11

---

[45] See note 12.
[46] Moynahan, *God's Bestseller*, p. xxii.

watched the burning of a young man in Norwich for possessing the Lord's prayer in English. … John Foxe records … seven Lollards burned at Coventry in 1519 for teaching their children the Lord's Prayer in English.'[47]

The burning fury of More

Tyndale hoped to escape this condemnation by getting official authorization for his translation in 1524. But he found just the opposite and had to escape from London to the continent where he did all his translating and writing for the next twelve years. He lived as a fugitive the entire time until his death near Brussels in 1536.

He watched a rising tide of persecution and felt the pain of seeing young men burned alive who were converted by reading his translation and his books. His closest friend, John Frith, was arrested in London and tried by Thomas More and burned alive July 4, 1531, at the age of twenty-eight. Richard Bayfield ran the ships that took Tyndale's books to England. He was betrayed and arrested, and Thomas More wrote on December 4, 1531, that Bayfield 'the monk and apostate [was] well and worthily burned in Smythfelde'.[48]

Three weeks later the same end came to John Tewkesbury. He was converted by reading Tyndale's *Parable of the Wicked Mammon* which defended justification by faith alone. He was whipped in Thomas More's garden and had his brow

---

[47] William Tyndale, *The Obedience of a Christian Man*, edited with an introduction by David Daniell (London: Penguin Books, 2000), p. 202.

[48] Moynahan, *God's Bestseller*, p. 260.

squeezed with small ropes till blood came out of his eyes. Then he was sent to the Tower where he was racked till he was lame. Then at last they burned him alive. Thomas More 'rejoiced that his victim was now in hell, where Tyndale "is like to find him when they come together"'.[49]

Four months later James Bainham followed in the flames in April of 1532. He had stood up during the mass at St Augustine's Church in London, lifted a copy of Tyndale's New Testament and pleaded with the people to die rather than deny the word of God. That virtually was to sign his own death warrant. Add to these Thomas Bilney, Thomas Dusgate, John Bent, Thomas Harding, Andrew Hewet, Elizabeth Barton and others, all burned alive for sharing the views of William Tyndale about the Scriptures and the reformed faith.[50]

Why so much hatred?

Why this extraordinary hostility against the English New Testament, especially from Thomas More who vilified Tyndale repeatedly in his denunciation of the reformers he burned? Some would say that the New Testament in English was rejected because it was accompanied with Reformation notes that the church regarded as heretical. That was true of later versions, but not the first 1526 edition. It did not have notes, and this is the edition that Bishop Tunstall had

[49] *Ibid.*, p. 261.
[50] The list and details are given in Daniell, *Tyndale*, pp. 183-184.

burned in London.[51] The church burned the word of God. It shocked Tyndale.

There were surface reasons and deeper reasons why the church opposed an English Bible. The surface reasons were that the English language is rude[52] and unworthy of the exalted language of God's word; and when one translates, errors can creep in, so it is safer not to translate; moreover, if the Bible is in English, then each man will become his own interpreter, and many will go astray into heresy and be condemned; and it was church tradition that only priests are given the divine grace to understand the Scriptures; and what's more, there is a special sacramental value to the Latin service in which people cannot understand, but grace is given. Such were the kinds of things being said on the surface.

But there were deeper reasons why the church opposed the English Bible: one doctrinal and one ecclesiastical. The church realized that they would not be able to sustain certain doctrines biblically because the people would see that they are not in the Bible. And the church realized that their power and control over the people, and even over the state, would be lost if certain doctrines were exposed as unbiblical—especially the priesthood and purgatory and penance.

The Bible must not be available for interpretation

Thomas More's criticism of Tyndale boils down mainly to the way Tyndale translated five words. He translated *presbuteros* as

---

[51] Daniell, *Tyndale*, pp. 192-193.
[52] Rough.

elder instead of priest. He translated *ekklesia* as congregation instead of church. He translated *metanoeo* as repent instead of do penance. He translated *exomologeo* as acknowledge or admit instead of confess. And he translated *agape* as love rather than charity.

Daniell comments, 'He cannot possibly have been unaware that those words in particular undercut the entire sacramental structure of the thousand year church throughout Europe, Asia and North Africa. It was the Greek New Testament that was doing the undercutting.'[53] And with the doctrinal undermining of these ecclesiastical pillars of priesthood and penance and confession, the pervasive power and control of the church collapsed. England would not be a Catholic nation. The reformed faith would flourish there in due time.

The sorrows and sufferings of a young fugitive

What did it cost William Tyndale under these hostile circumstances to stay faithful to his calling as a translator of the Bible and a writer of the reformed faith?

He fled his homeland in 1524 and was killed in 1536. He gives us some glimpse of those twelve years as a fugitive in Germany and the Netherlands in one of the very few personal descriptions we have from Stephen Vaughan's letter in 1531. He refers to

> … my pains … my poverty … my exile out of mine natural country, and bitter absence from my friends . . . my hunger,

[53] *Ibid.*, p. 149.

my thirst, my cold, the great danger wherewith I am everywhere encompassed, and finally ... innumerable other hard and sharp fightings which I endure.[54]

All these sufferings came to a climax on May 21, 1535, in the midst of Tyndale's great Old Testament translation labours. We can feel some of the ugliness of what happened in the words of David Daniell: 'Malice, self-pity, villainy and deceit were about to destroy everything. These evils came to the English House [in Antwerp], wholly uninvited, in the form of an egregious Englishman, Henry Philips.'[55] Philips had won Tyndale's trust over some months and then betrayed him. John Foxe tells how it happened:

So when it was dinner-time, Master Tyndale went forth with Philips, and at the going forth of Poyntz's house, was a long narrow entry, so that two could not go in a front. Mr Tyndale would have put Philips before him, but Philips would in no wise, but put Master Tyndale before, for that he pretended to show great humanity. So Master Tyndale, being a man of no great stature, went before, and Philips, a tall comely person, followed behind him: who had set officers on either side of the door upon two seats, who, being there, might see who came in the entry: and coming through the same entry, Philips pointed with his finger over Master Tyndale's head down to him, that the officers who sat at the door might see that it was he whom they should take. ... Then they took him, and brought him to the emperor's attorney, or procurer-general,

54 *Ibid.*, p. 213.
55 *Ibid.*, p. 361.

where he dined. Then came the procurer-general to the house of Poyntz, and sent away all that was there of Master Tyndale's, as well his books as other things: and from thence Tyndale was had to the castle of Filford, eighteen English miles from Antwerp, and there he remained until he was put to death.[56]

The cold and final castle

Vilvorde Castle is six miles north of Brussels and about the same distance from Louvain. Here Tyndale stayed for 18 months. 'The charge was heresy, with not agreeing with the Holy Roman Emperor—in a nutshell, being Lutheran.'[57] A four-man commission from the Catholic centre of Louvain was authorized to prove that Tyndale was a heretic. One of them named Latomus filled three books with his interactions with Tyndale and said that Tyndale himself wrote a 'book' in prison to defend his chief doctrinal standard: *Sola fides justificat apud Deum—Faith Alone Justifies Before God.* This was the key issue in the end. The evil of translating the Bible came down to this: are we justified by faith alone?

These months in prison were not easy. They were a long dying leading to death. We get one glimpse into the prison to see Tyndale's condition and his passion. He wrote a letter in September, 1535, when there seems to have been a lull in the examinations. It was addressed to an unnamed officer of the castle. Here is a condensed version of Mozley's translation of the Latin:

[56] *Ibid.*, p. 364.
[57] *Ibid.*, p. 365.

I beg your lordship, and that of the Lord Jesus, that if I am to remain here through the winter, you will request the commissary to have the kindness to send me, from the goods of mine which he has, a warmer cap; for I suffer greatly from cold in the head, and am afflicted by a perpetual catarrh, which is much increased in this cell; a warmer coat also, for this which I have is very thin; a piece of cloth too to patch my leggings. My overcoat is worn out; my shirts are also worn out. He has a woollen shirt, if he will be good enough to send it. I have also with him leggings of thicker cloth to put on above; he has also warmer night-caps. And I ask to be allowed to have a lamp in the evening; it is indeed wearisome sitting alone in the dark. But most of all I beg and beseech your clemency to be urgent with the commissary, that he will kindly permit me to have the Hebrew Bible, Hebrew grammar, and Hebrew dictionary, that I may pass the time in that study. In return may you obtain what you most desire, so only that it be for the salvation of your soul. But if any other decision has been taken concerning me, to be carried out before winter, I will be patient, abiding the will of God, to the glory of the grace of my Lord Jesus Christ: whose spirit (I pray) may ever direct your heart. Amen W. Tindalus.[58]

We don't know if his requests were granted. He did stay in that prison through the winter. His verdict was sealed in August, 1536. He was formally condemned as a heretic and degraded from the priesthood. Then in early October (traditionally October 6), he was tied to the stake and then

[58] *Ibid.*, p. 379.

strangled by the executioner, then afterward consumed in the fire. Foxe reports that his last words were, 'Lord! Open the King of England's eyes!'[59] He was forty-two years old, never married and never buried.

He will ease your pain or shorten it

I conclude by drawing attention to some words taken from his book *The Obedience of a Christian Man*:

> If God promise riches, the way thereto is poverty. Whom he loveth he chasteneth, whom he exalteth, he casteth down, whom he saveth he damneth first, he bringeth no man to heaven except he send him to hell first. If he promise life he slayeth it first, when he buildeth, he casteth all down first. He is no patcher, he cannot build on another man's foundation. He will not work until all be past remedy and brought unto such a case, that men may see how that his hand, his power, his mercy, his goodness and truth hath wrought all together. He will let no man be partaker with him of his praise and glory.[60]

> Let us therefore look diligently whereunto we are called, that we deceive not ourselves. We are called, not to dispute as the pope's disciples do, but to die with Christ that we may live with him, and to suffer with him that we may reign with him.[61]

---

[59] *Ibid.*, pp. 382-383. 'Contemporaries noted no such words, however, only that the strangling was bungled and that he suffered terribly.' Moynahan, *God's Best-seller*, p. 377.

[60] Tyndale, *The Obedience of a Christian Man*, p. 6.

[61] *Ibid.*, p. 8.

For if God be on our side: what matter maketh it who be against us, be they bishops, cardinals, popes or whatsoever names they will.[62]

So let Tyndale's very last word to us be the last word he sent to his best friend, John Frith, in a letter just before he was burned alive for believing and speaking the truth of Scripture:

> Your cause is Christ's gospel, a light that must be fed with the blood of faith. … If when we be buffeted for well-doing, we suffer patiently and endure, that is thankful with God; for to that end we are called. For Christ also suffered for us, leaving us an example that we should follow his steps, who did no sin. Hereby have we perceived love that he laid down his life for us: therefore we ought to be able to lay down our lives for the brethren. … Let not your body faint. If the pain be above your strength, remember: 'Whatsoever ye shall ask in my name, I will give it you.' And pray to our Father in that name, and he will ease your pain, or shorten it. … Amen.

[62] *Ibid.*, p. 6.

AN EXTRACT FROM TYNDALE'S

An Answer to Sir Thomas More's Dialogue

What the church is

This word church hath divers significations. First it signifieth a place or house; whither Christian people were wont in the old time to resort at times convenient, for to hear the word of doctrine, the law of God, and the faith of our Saviour Jesus Christ, and how and what to pray, and whence to ask power and strength to live godly. For the officer, thereto appointed, preached the pure word of God only, and prayed in a tongue that all men understood: and the people hearkened unto his prayers, and said thereto Amen; and prayed with him in their hearts, and of him learned to pray at home and everywhere, and to instruct every man his household.

Where now we hear but voices without significations, and buzzings, howlings, and cryings, as it were the hallooing of foxes, or baitings of bears; and wonder at disguisings and toys, whereof we know no meaning. By reason whereof we be fallen into such ignorance, that we know of the mercy and promises, which are in Christ, nothing at all. And of the law of God we think as do the Turks, and as did the old heathen people; how that it is a thing which every man may do of his own power, and in doing thereof becometh good, and waxeth righteous, and deserveth heaven; yea, and are yet more mad than that: for we imagine the same of fantasies, and vain ceremonies of our own making; neither needful unto the taming of our own flesh, neither profitable unto our neighbour, neither honour unto God. And of prayer we think, that no man can pray but at church; and that it is nothing else but to say *Pater noster* unto a post: wherewith yet, and with other observances of our own imagining, we believe we deserve to be sped of all that our blind hearts desire.

In another signification, it is abused and mistaken for a multitude of shaven, shorn, and oiled; which we now call the spiritualty and clergy. As when we read in the chronicles, 'King William was a great tyrant, and a wicked man unto holy church, and took much lands from them.' 'King John was also a perilous man and a wicked unto holy church; and would have had them punished for theft, murder, and whatsoever mischief they did, as though they had not been people anointed, but even of the vile rascal and common lay-people.' And, 'Thomas Becket was a blessed and an holy man; for he died for the liberties (to do all mischief unpunished) and privileges of the church.' 'Is he a layman, or a man of the church?' 'Such is the living of holy church.' 'So men say of holy church.' 'Ye must believe in holy church, and do as they teach you.' 'Will ye not obey holy church?' 'Will ye not do the penance enjoined you by holy church?' 'Will ye not forswear obedience unto holy church?' 'Beware lest ye fall into the indignation of holy church, lest they curse you'; and so forth. In which all, we understand but the pope, cardinals, legates, patriarchs, archbishops, bishops, abbots, priors, chancellors, archdeacons, commissaries, officials, priests, monks, friars, black, white, pied, grey, and so forth, by (I trow) a thousand names of blasphemy and of hypocrisies, and as many sundry fashions of disguisings.

It hath yet, or should have, another signification, little known among the common people nowadays. That is to wit, it signifieth a congregation; a multitude or a company gathered together in one, of all degrees of people. As a man would say, 'the church of London', meaning not the spiritualty only (as they will be called for their diligent serving of God in the spirit, and so sore eschewing to meddle with temporal matters), but the whole body of the city, of all kinds, conditions, and degrees: and 'the church of Bristow'[1] all that pertain unto that town generally. And what congregation is meant, thou shalt alway understand by the matter that is entreated of, and by the circumstances thereof. And in this third signification is the church of God, or Christ, taken in the scripture; even for the whole multitude of all them that receive the name of Christ to believe in him, and not for the

---

[1] Bristol.

clergy only. For Paul saith (Galatians 1), 'I persecuted the church of God above measure': which was not the preachers only, but all that believed generally: as it is to see Acts 22 where he saith: 'I persecuted this way even unto the death, binding and putting in prison both men and women.' And (Galatians 1), 'I was unknown concerning my person unto the congregations of the Jews which were in Christ.' And (Rom. 16), 'I commend unto you Phoebe, the deaconess of the church of Cenchris.' And, 'The churches of Asia salute you' (1 Cor. the last). And, 'If a man cannot rule his own house, how shall he take the care of the church of God?' 'If any faithful man or woman have widows, let them find them, that the church be not charged.' And, 'If thy brother hear thee not, tell the church or congregation'; and so forth. In which places, and throughout all the scripture, the church is taken for the whole multitude of them that believe in Christ in that place, in that parish, town, city, province, land, or throughout all the world, and not for the spiritualty only.

Notwithstanding yet it is sometimes taken generally for all them that embrace the name of Christ, though their faiths be naught, or though they have no faith at all. And sometimes it is taken specially for the elect only; in whose hearts God hath written his law with his holy Spirit, and given them a feeling faith of the mercy that is in Christ Jesu our Lord.

Why Tyndale used this word congregation, *rather than* church, *in the translation of the New Testament*

Wherefore, inasmuch as the clergy (as the nature of those hard and indurate adamant stones is, to draw all to them) had appropriate unto themselves the term that of right is common unto all the whole congregation of them that believe in Christ; and with their false and subtle wiles had beguiled and mocked the people, and brought them into the ignorance of the word; making them understand by this word *church* nothing but the shaven flock of them that shore the whole world; therefore in the translation of the New Testament, where I found this word *ecclesia*, I interpreted it by this word *congregation*. Even therefore did I it, and not of any mischievous mind or purpose to stablish heresy, as Master More untruly reporteth of me in his dialogue, where he raileth on the translation of the New Testament.

And when M. More saith, that this word *church* is known well enough, I report me unto the consciences of all the land, whether he say truth or otherwise; or whether the lay-people understand by *church* the whole multitude of all that profess Christ, or the juggling spirits only. And when he saith that *congregation* is a more general term; if it were, it hurteth not: for the circumstance doth ever tell what congregation is meant. Nevertheless yet saith he not the truth. For wheresoever I may say a *congregation*, there may I say a *church* also; as the church of the devil, the church of Satan, the church of wretches, the church of wicked men, the church of liars, and a church of Turks thereto. For M. More must grant (if he will have *ecclesia* translated throughout all the New Testament by this word *church*) that *church* is as common as *ecclesia*. Now is *ecclesia* a Greek word, and was in use before the time of the apostles, and taken for a congregation among the heathen, where was no congregation of God or of Christ. And also Luke himself useth *ecclesia* for a church, or congregation, of heathen people thrice in one chapter, even in the nineteenth chapter of the Acts, where Demetrius the goldsmith, or silversmith, had gathered a company against Paul for preaching against images.

Howbeit, M. More hath so long used his figures of poetry, that (I suppose) when he erreth most, he now, by the reason of a long custom, believeth himself that he saith most true. Or else, as the wise people, which when they dance naked in nets, believe that no man seeth them; even so M. More thinketh that his errors be so subtly couched that no man can espy them. So blind he counteth all other men, in comparison of his great understanding. But charitably I exhort him in Christ to take heed; for though Judas were wilier than his fellows to get lucre, yet he proved not most wise at the last end. Neither though Baalam, the false prophet, had a clear sight to bring the curse of God upon the children of Israel for honour's sake; yet his covetousness did so blind his prophecy, that he could not see his own end. Let, therefore, M. More and his company awake by times, ere ever their sin be ripe; lest the voice of their wickedness ascend up, and awake God out of his sleep, to look upon them, and to bow his ears unto their cursed blasphemies against the open truth, and to send his harvestmen and mowers of vengeance to reap it.

But how happeth it that M. More hath not contended in like wise against his darling Erasmus all this long while? Doth he not change this word *ecclesia* into *congregation*, and that not seldom in the New Testament?[1] Peradventure he oweth him favour, because he made *Moria* in his house:[2] which book, if it were in English, then should every man see how that he then was far otherwise minded than he now writeth. But, verily, I think that as Judas betrayed not Christ for any love that he had unto the high priests, scribes and Pharisees, but only to come by that wherefore he thirsted; even so M. More (as there are tokens evident) wrote not these books for any affection that he bare unto the spiritualty, or unto the opinions which he so barely defendeth, but to obtain only that which he was an hungred for. I pray God that he eat not too hastily, lest he be choked at the latter end; but that he repent, and resist not the Spirit of God, which openeth light unto the world.

Why he useth this word elder, *and not* priest

Another thing which he rebuketh is, that I interpret this Greek word *presbyteros* by this word *senior*. Of a truth *senior*

---

[1] Erasmus has rendered it *congregation* in his version of Acts 2:47; 5:11; 11:26; Rom. 16:5; 1 Cor. 14:4; Col. 4:15; Philem. 2. And in Acts 19:4 and Heb. 12:23 he has rendered *ecclesia, concio.*

[2] Erasmus' celebrated satirical production, the *Encomium Moriae*; in which he held up to ridicule the ignorance frequent among the popish clergy and the friars.

is no very good English, though senior and junior be used in the universities; but there came no better in my mind at that time. Howbeit, I spied my fault since, long ere M. More told it me, and have mended it in all the works which I since made, and call it an *elder*. And in that he maketh heresy of it, to call *presbyteros* an *elder*, he condemneth their own old Latin text of heresy, which only they use yet daily in the church, and have used, I suppose, this fourteen hundred years: for that text doth call it *an elder* likewise. In the 1 Pet. 5 thus standeth it in the Latin text: *Seniores ergo qui in vobis sunt obsecro consenior, pascite qui in vobis est gregem Christi*: 'The elders that are among you, I beseech, which am an elder also, that ye feed the flock of Christ, which is among you.' There is *presbyteros* called an *elder*. And in that he saith, 'Feed Christ's flock', he meaneth even the ministers that were chosen to teach the people, and to inform them in God's word, and no lay persons. And in the second epistle of John saith the text, *Senior electae dominae et filiis ejus*: 'The elder unto the elect lady and to her children.' And in the third epistle of John, *Senior Gaio dilecto*: 'The elder unto the beloved Gaius.' In these two epistles *presbyteros* is called an *elder*. And in Acts, chap. 20, the text saith: 'Paul sent for *majores natu ecclesiae*, the elders in birth of the congregation or church, and said unto them, Take heed unto yourselves, and unto the whole flock, over which the Holy Ghost hath made you *episcopos ad regendum ecclesiam Dei*', bishops, or overseers, to govern the church of God. There is *presbyteros* called an *elder in birth*;

which same immediately is called a bishop or overseer, to declare what persons are meant. Hereof ye see that I have no more erred than their own text, which they have used since the scripture was first in the Latin tongue, and that their own text understandeth by *presbyteros* nothing save an *elder*. And they were called elders, because of their age, gravity and sadness, as thou mayest see by the text; and bishops, or overseers, by the reason of their offices. And all that were called elders (or priests, if they so will) were called bishops also, though they have divided the names now: which thing thou mayest evidently see by the first chapter of Titus, and Acts 20, and other places more.

And when he layeth Timothy unto my charge, how he was young, then he weeneth that he hath won his gilden spurs.[1] But I would pray him to shew me where he readeth that Paul calleth him *presbyteros*, priest or elder. I durst not then call him *episcopus* properly: for those overseers, which we now call bishops after the Greek word, were alway biding in one place, to govern the congregation there. Now was Timothy an apostle. And Paul also writeth that he came shortly again. Well, will he say, it cometh yet all to one; for if it becometh the lower minister to be of a sad and discreet age, much more it becometh the higher. It is truth. But two things are without law, God and necessity. If God, to shew his power, shall shed out his grace more upon youth than upon age at a

---

[1] A person capable of receiving knighthood was said to have won his spurs, when he had made himself so conspicuous in the field of battle as to ensure his being knighted.

time, who shall let[1] him? Women be no meet vessels to rule or to preach, for both are forbidden them; yet hath God endowed them with his Spirit at sundry times, and shewed his power and goodness upon them, and wrought wonderful things by them, because he would not have them despised. We read that women have judged all Israel, and have been great prophetesses, and have done mighty deeds. Yea, and if stories be true, women have preached since the opening of the New Testament. Do not our women now christen and minister the sacrament of baptism in time of need? Might they not, by as good reason, preach also, if necessity required? If a woman were driven into some island, where Christ was never preached, might she there not preach him, if she had the gift thereto? Might she not also baptize? And why might she not, by the same reason, minister the sacrament of the body and blood of Christ, and teach them how to choose officers and ministers? O poor women, how despise ye them! The viler the better welcome unto you. An whore had ye lever[2] than an honest wife. If only shaven and anointed may do these things, then Christ did them not, nor any of his apostles, nor any man in long time after: for they used no such ceremonies.

Notwithstanding, though God be under no law, and necessity lawless; yet be we under a law, and ought to prefer the men before the women, and age before youth, as nigh as we can. For it is against the law of nature that young men

[1] That is, hinder.
[2] Raise.

should rule the elder, and as uncomely as that women should rule the men, but when need requireth. And therefore, if Paul had had other shift, and a man of age as meet for the room, he would not have put Timothy in the office; he should no doubt have been kept back until a fuller age, and have learned in the meantime in silence. And whatsoever thou be that readest this, I exhort thee in our Lord that thou read both the epistles of Paul to Timothy; that thou mayest see how diligently (as a mother careth for her child, if it be in peril) Paul writeth unto Timothy, to instruct him, to teach him, to exhort, to courage him, to stir him up to be wise, sober, diligent, circumspect, sad,[1] humble and meek, saying: 'These I write that thou mayest know how to behave thyself in the house of God, which is the church' or congregation. Avoid lusts of youth, beware of ungodly fables and old wives' tales; and avoid the company of men of corrupt minds, which waste their brains about wrangling questions. 'Let no man despise thine youth.' As who shall say, 'Youth is a despised thing of itself; whereunto men give none obedience naturally or reverence. See, therefore, that thy virtue exceed, to recompense thy lack of age; and that thou so behave thyself that no fault be found with thee.' And again, 'Rebuke not an elder sharply, but exhort him as thy father, and young men as thy brethren, and the elder women as thy mothers, and the young women as thy sisters'; and such like in every chapter. 'Admit none accusation against an elder, under less

[1] Grave, serious.

than two witnesses.' And Paul chargeth him 'in the sight of God and of the Lord Jesus Christ, and of his elect angels, to do nothing rashly', or of affection. And shortly, whereunto youth is most prone and ready to fall, thereof warneth he him with all diligence, even almost or altogether half a dozen times of some one thing. And finally, as a man would teach a child that had never before gone to school, so tenderly and so carefully doth Paul teach him. It is another thing to teach the people, and to teach the preacher. Here Paul teacheth the preacher, young Timothy.

And when he affirmeth that I say, how that the oiling and shaving is no part of the priesthood,[1] that improveth he not, nor can do. And therefore I say it yet. And when he hath insearched the uttermost that he can, this is all that he can lay against me, that of an hundred there be not ten that have the properties which Paul requireth to be in them. Wherefore, if oiling and shaving be no part of their priesthood, then evermore of a thousand nine hundred at the least should be no priests at all. And 'Quoth your friend'[2] would confirm it with an oath, and swear deeply, that it would follow, and that it must needs so be: which argument yet, if there were no other shift, I would solve after an Oxford fashion, with *Goncedo consequentiam et consequens*.[3] And I say moreover,

---

[1] 'The name of priest which to us, in our own tongue, hath always signified an anointed person, and with holy orders consecrated unto God, he hath changed.' More's Dial.

[2] Tyndale's ironical name for a speaker in More's Dialogue.

[3] I concede the consequence and whatever is deducible.

that their anointing is but a ceremony borrowed of the Jews, though they have somewhat altered the manner; and their shaving borrowed of the heathen priests; and that they be no more of their priesthood, than the oil, salt, spittle, taper and chrisom-cloth, of the substance of baptism. Which things, no doubt, because they be of their conjuring, they would have preached of necessity unto the salvation of the child, except necessity had driven them unto the contrary. And seeing that the oil is not of necessity, let M. More tell me what more virtue is in the oil of confirmation, inasmuch as the bishop sacreth the one as well as the other; yea, and let him tell the reason why there should be more virtue in the oil wherewith the bishop anointeth his priests. Let him tell you from whence the oil cometh, how it is made, and why he selleth it to the curates wherewith they anoint the sick, or whether this be of less virtue than the other.

And finally, why used not the apostles this Greek word *hiereus*, or the interpreter this Latin word *sacerdos*, but alway this word *presbyteros* and *senior*, by which was at that time nothing signified but an *elder*? And it was no doubt taken of the custom of the Hebrews, where the officers were ever elderly men, as nature requireth: as it appeareth in the Old Testament, and also in the New. 'The scribes, Pharisees, and the elders of the people', saith the text; which were the officers and rulers, so called by the reason of their age.

Why he useth love, *rather than* charity

He rebuketh me also that I translate this Greek word *agape* into *love*, and not rather into *charity*, so holy and so known a term. Verily, *charity* is no known English, in that sense which *agape* requireth. For when we say, 'Give your alms in the worship of God, and sweet St Charity'; and when the father teacheth his son to say, 'Blessing, father, for St Charity'; what mean they? In good faith they wot[1] not. Moreover, when we say, 'God help you, I have done my charity for this day', do we not take it for alms? and, 'The man is ever chiding and out of charity'; and, 'I beshrew[2] him, saving my charity'; there we take it for patience. And when I say, 'A charitable man', it is taken for merciful. And though mercifulness be a good love, or rather spring of a good love, yet is not every good love mercifulness. As when a woman loveth her husband godly, or a man his wife or his friend that is in none adversity, it is not always mercifulness. Also we say not, This man hath a great charity to God; but a great love. Wherefore I must have used this general term *love* in spite of mine heart oftentimes. And *agape* and *caritas* were words used among the heathen, ere Christ came; and signified therefore more than a godly love. And we may say well enough, and have heard it spoken, that the Turks be charitable one to another among themselves, and some of them unto the Christians too. Besides all this, *agape* is common unto all loves.

[1] Know.
[2] Curse.

And when M. More saith, 'Every love is not charity';[1] no more is every apostle Christ's apostle; nor every angel God's angel; nor every hope Christian hope; nor every faith, or belief, Christ's belief; and so by an hundred thousand words: so that if I should always use but a word that were no more general than the word I interpret, I should interpret nothing at all. But the matter itself and the circumstances do declare what love, what hope, and what faith is spoken of. And, finally, I say not, charity God, or charity your neighbour; but, love God, and love your neighbour; yea, and though we say a man ought to love his neighbour's wife and his daughter, a Christian man doth not understand that he is commanded to defile his neighbour's wife or his neighbour's daughter.

Why favour, *and not* grace

And with like reasons rageth he, because I turn *charis* into *favour*, and not into *grace*: saying that 'every favour is not grace, and that in some favour there is but little grace'. I can say also, 'in some grace there is little goodness'; and when we say 'he standeth well in my lady's grace', we understand no great godly favour. And in universities many ungracious graces there be gotten.[2]

---

[1] 'Charity signifieth, in Englishmen's ears, not every common love, but a good, virtuous, and well-ordered love.' More's Dial.

[2] The passing of any resolution by the ruling body for the conferring of a degree is called passing a grace, in the university of Cambridge.

Why knowledge, *and not* confession; repentance, *and not* penance

And that I use this word *knowledge*, and not *confession*; and this word *repentance*, and not *penance*.[1] In which all he cannot prove that I give not the right English unto the Greek word. But it is a far other thing that paineth them, and biteth them by the breasts. There be secret pangs that pinch the very hearts of them, whereof they dare not complain. The sickness, that maketh them so impatient, is that they have lost their juggling terms. For the doctors and preachers were wont to make many divisions, distinctions, and sorts of grace; *gratis data*, *gratum faciens*, *prœveniens*, and *subsequens*.[2] And with confession they juggled; and so made the people, as oft as they spake of it, understand *shrift in the ear*;[3] whereof the scripture maketh no mention: no, it is clean against the scripture, as they use it and preach it; and unto God an abomination, and a foul stinking sacrifice unto the filthy idol Priapus.[4] The loss of those juggling terms is the matter whereof all these bots[5] breed; that gnaw them by the bellies, and make them so unquiet.

And in like manner, by this word *penance* they make the people understand holy deeds of their enjoining; with which

---

[1] 'Confession he translateth into knowledge: penance into repentance; a contrite heart he changeth into a troubled heart.' More's Dial. Tyndale frequently uses *knowledge* for *acknowledge*.

[2] Freely given: making acceptable; going before; and following after.

[3] The Roman Catholic practice of a priest hearing confession and giving absolution.

[4] In Greek mythology Priapus was a minor rustic fertility god who was thought to protect livestock, fruit plants, and male genitalia. He was later regarded as the chief god of lasciviousness and sensuality.

[5] Maggots.

they must make satisfaction unto God-ward for their sins: when all the scripture preacheth that Christ hath made full satisfaction for our sins to God-ward; and we must now be thankful to God again, and kill the lusts of our flesh with holy works of God's enjoining. And I am bound to take patiently all that God layeth on my back; and, if I have hurt my neighbour, to shrive[1] myself unto him, and to make him amends, if I have wherewith; or if not, then to ask him forgiveness, and he is bound to forgive me. And as for their *penance*, the scripture knoweth not of [it]. The Greek hath *Metanoia*, and *Metanoite*, repentance and repent; or fore-thinking and forethink. As we say in English, 'It forethinketh me, or I forethink'; and 'I repent, or it repenteth me'; and 'I am sorry that I did it.' So now the scripture saith, 'Repent, or let it forethink you; and come and believe the gospel, or glad tidings, that is brought you in Christ, and so shall all be forgiven you; and henceforth live a new life.' And it will follow, if I repent in the heart, that I shall do no more so, willingly and of purpose. And if I believed the gospel, what God hath done for me in Christ, I should surely love him again, and of love prepare myself unto his commandments.

These things to be even so, M. More knoweth well enough: for he understandeth the Greek, and he knew them long ere I. But so blind is covetousness and drunken desire of honour. 'Gifts blind the eyes of the seeing, and pervert the words of the righteous' (Deut. 16). When covetousness findeth vantage in serving falsehood, it riseth up into an obstinate malice

[1] Confess my sins.

47

against the truth, and seeketh all means to resist it and to quench it: as Balaam the false prophet, though he wist[1] that God loved Israel, and had blessed them, and promised them great things, and that he would fulfil his promises; yet for covetousness and desire of honour he fell into such malice against the truth of God, that he sought how to resist it and to curse the people: which when God would not let him do, he turned himself another way, and gave pestilent counsel to make the people sin against God; whereby the wrath of God fell upon them, and many thousands perished. Notwithstanding God's truth abode fast, and was fulfilled in the rest. And Balaam, as he was the cause that many perished, so escaped he not himself. No more did any that maliciously resisted the open truth against his own conscience, since the world began, that ever I read. For it is sin against the Holy Ghost, which Christ saith shall neither be forgiven here, nor in the world to come: which text may this wise be understood, that as that sin shall be punished with everlasting damnation in the life to come, even so shall it not escape vengeance here; as thou seest in Judas, in Pharaoh, in Balaam, and in all other tyrants, which against their consciences resisted the open truth of God.

So now the cause why our prelates thus rage, and that moveth them to call M. More to help, is not that they find just causes in the translation, but because they have lost their juggling and feigned terms; wherewith Peter prophesied they should make merchandise of the people.

[1] Knew.

Whether the church were before the gospel, or the gospel before the church

Another doubt there is; whether the church or congregation be before the gospel, or the gospel before the church: which question is as hard to solve, as whether the father be elder than the son, or the son elder than his father. For the whole scripture, and all believing hearts, testify that we are begotten through the word. Wherefore, if the word beget the congregation, and he that begetteth is before him that is begotten, then is the gospel before the church. Paul also (Rom. 10) saith, 'How shall they call on him whom they believe not? And how shall they believe without a preacher?' That is, Christ must first be preached, ere men can believe in him. And then it followeth, that the word of the preacher must be before the faith of the believer. And therefore, inasmuch as the word is before the faith, and faith maketh the congregation, therefore is the word of the gospel before the congregation. And again, as the air is dark of itself, and receiveth all her light of the sun; even so are all men's hearts of themselves dark with lies, and receive all their truth of God's word, in that they consent thereto. And, moreover, as the dark air giveth the sun no light, but contrariwise the light of the sun in respect of the air is of itself, and lighteneth the air, and purgeth it from darkness: even so, the lying heart of man can give the word of God no truth; but, contrariwise, the truth of God's word is of herself, and lighteneth the hearts of the believers, and maketh them true, and cleanseth them from lies, as thou readest, John 15: 'Ye be clean by reason of the word.' Which is to be understood, in that the word had purged their hearts from lies, from false opinions, and from thinking evil good, and therefore from consenting to sin. And (John 17) 'Sanctify them, O Father, through thy truth: and thy word is truth.' And thus thou seest that God's truth dependeth not of man. It is not true because man so saith, or admitteth it for true: but man is true, because he believeth it, testifieth and giveth witness in his heart that it is true. And Christ also saith himself, (John 5) 'I receive no witness of man.' For if the multitude of man's witness might make aught true, then were the doctrine of Mahomet truer than Christ's.

Whether the apostles left aught unwritten, that is of necessity to be believed

But did not the apostles teach aught by mouth, that they wrote not? I answer, because that many taught one thing, and every man the same in divers places, and unto divers people, and confirmed every sermon with a sundry miracle; therefore Christ and his apostles preached an hundred thousand sermons, and did as many miracles, which had been superfluous to have been all written. But the pith and substance in general of every thing necessary unto our souls' health, both of what we ought to believe, and what we ought to do, was written; and of the miracles done to confirm it, as many as were needful: so that whatsoever we ought to believe or do, that same is written expressly, or drawn out of that which is written.

For if I were bound to do or believe, under pain of the loss of my soul, anything that were not written, nor depended of that which is written, what holp[1] me the scripture that is written? And thereto, inasmuch as Christ and all his apostles warned us that false prophets should come with false miracles, even to deceive the elect if it were possible; wherewith should the true preacher confound the false, except he brought true miracles to confound the false, or else authentic scripture, of full authority already among the people?

Some man would ask, How did God continue his congregation from Adam to Noah, and from Noah to Abraham, and so to Moses, without writing, but with teaching from mouth to mouth? I answer, first, that there was no scripture all the while, they shall prove when our lady hath a new son. God taught Adam greater things than to write. And that there was writing in the world long ere Abraham, yea and ere Noah, do stories testify.[2] Notwithstanding, though there had been no writing, the preachers were ever prophets, glorious in doing of miracles, wherewith they confirmed their preaching. And beyond that, God wrote his testament unto them alway, both what to do and to believe, even in sacraments. For the sacrifices which God gave Adam's sons were no dumb popetry[3] or superstitious mahometry, but signs of the testament of God. And in them they read the word of God, as we do in books; and as we should do in our sacraments, if

---

[1] From old English word 'holpen'; what help to me is the scripture that is written?

[2] He was doubtless led to say this by believing Josephus' tale about the pillars of Seth. Hist. Jud. L. 1. c. 2.

[3] Popetrie, or puppetry.

the wicked pope had not taken the significations away from us, as he hath robbed us of the true sense of all the scripture. The testament which God made with Noah, that he would no more drown the world with water, he wrote in the sacrament of the rainbow. And the appointment made between him and Abraham he wrote in the sacrament of circumcision. And therefore said Stephen (Acts 7), 'He gave them the testament of circumcision': not that the outward circumcision was the whole testament, but the sacrament or sign thereof. For circumcision preached God's word unto them, as I have in other places declared.

But in the time of Moses, when the congregation was in- creased, that they must have many preachers, and also rulers temporal, then all was received in scripture; insomuch that Christ and his apostles might not have been believed without scripture, for all their miracles. Wherefore, inasmuch as Christ's congregation is spread abroad into all the world, much broader than Moses'; and inasmuch as we have not the Old Testament only, but also the New, wherein all things are opened so richly, and all fulfilled that before was promised; and inasmuch as there is no promise behind of aught to be shewed more, save the resurrection; yea, and seeing that Christ and all the apostles, with all the angels of heaven, if they were here, could preach no more than is preached, of necessity unto our souls: how then should we receive a new article of the faith, without scripture, as profitable unto my soul, when I had believed it, as smoke for sore eyes? What holp it me to believe that our lady's body is in heaven? What am I the better for the belief of purgatory? To fear[1] men, thou wilt say. Christ and his apostles thought hell enough. And yet (besides that the fleshly imagination may not stand with God's word) what great fear can there be of that terrible fire, which thou mayest quench almost for three half-pence? And that the apostles should teach aught by mouth which they would not write, I pray you for what purpose? Because they should not come into the hands of the heathen for mocking, saith M. More. I pray you, what thing more to be mocked of the heathen could they teach, than the resurrection; and that Christ was God and man, and died between two thieves; and that for his death's sake all that repent, and believe therein, should have their sins forgiven them? Yea, and if the apostles understood thereby as we do, what madder thing unto heathen people could they have taught than that bread is Christ's body, and wine his blood? And yet all these things they wrote. And again, purgatory, confession in the ear, penance and satisfaction for sin to God-ward, with holy deeds, and praying to saints, with such like, as dumb sacraments and ceremonies, are marvellous agreeable unto the superstition of the heathen people; so that they needed not to abstain from writing of them, for fear lest the heathen should have mocked them.

Moreover, what is it that the apostles taught by mouth, and durst not write? The sacraments? As for baptism, and

---

[1] 'To make men fear'.

the sacrament of the body and blood of Christ, they wrote, and it is expressed what is signified by them. And also all the ceremonies and sacraments that were from Adam to Christ had significations; and all that are made mention of in the New Testament. Wherefore, inasmuch as the sacraments of the Old Testament have significations; and inasmuch as the sacraments of the New Testament (of which mention is made that they were delivered unto us by the very apostles, at Christ's commandment) have also significations; and inasmuch as the office of an apostle is to edify in Christ; and inasmuch as a dumb ceremony edifieth not, but hurteth altogether (for if it preach not unto me, then I cannot but put confidence therein that the deed itself justifieth me, which is the denying of Christ's blood); and inasmuch as no mention is made of them, as well as of other, nor is known what is meant by them; therefore it appeareth that the apostles taught them not, but that they be the false merchandise of wily hypocrites. And thereto, priesthood was, in the time of the apostles, an office, which if they would do truly, it would more profit than all the sacraments in the world. And again, God's holinesses strive not one against another, nor defile one another. Their sacraments defile one another: for wedlock defileth priesthood more than whoredom, theft, murder, or any sin against nature.

They will haply demand where it is written, that women should baptize? Verily, in this commandment, 'Love thy neighbour as thyself', it is written that they may and ought to minister not only baptism, but all other sacraments also in time of need, if they be so necessary as they preach them.

And finally, though we were sure that God himself had given us a sacrament, whatsoever it were, yet if the signification were once lost, we must of necessity either seek up the signification, or put some signification of God's word thereto, what we ought to do or believe thereby, or else put it down. For it is impossible to observe a sacrament, without signification, but unto our damnation. If we keep the faith purely and the law of love undefiled, which are the significations of all ceremonies, there is no jeopardy to alter or change the fashion of the ceremony, or to put it down, if need require.

Whether the church can err

There is another question, whether the church may err. Which if ye understand of the pope and his generation, it is verily as hard a question as to ask whether he which had both his eyes out be blind or no; or whether it be possible for him that hath one leg shorter than another to halt. But I said that Christ's elect church is the whole multitude of all repenting sinners that believe in Christ, and put all their trust and confidence in the mercy of God; feeling in their hearts that God for Christ's sake loveth them, and will be, or rather is, merciful unto them, and forgiveth them their sins of which they repent; and that he forgiveth them also all the motions unto sin, of which they fear lest they should thereby be drawn into sin again. And this faith they have without all respect of their own deservings, yea, and for none other cause than that the merciful truth of God the Father, which cannot lie, hath so promised and so sworn.

And this faith and knowledge is everlasting life; and by this we be born anew, and made the sons of God, and obtain forgiveness of sins, and are translated from death to life, and from the wrath of God unto his love and favour. And this faith is the mother of all truth, and bringeth with her the Spirit of all truth; which Spirit purgeth us, as from all sin, even so from all lies and error, noisome and hurtful. And this faith is the foundation laid of the apostles and prophets; whereon Paul saith (Eph. 2) that we are built, and thereby of the household of God. And this faith is the rock, whereon Christ built his congregation. Christ asked the apostles (Matt. 16) whom they took him for. And Peter answered for them all, saying, 'I say that thou art Christ, the Son of the living God, that art come into this world.' That is, We believe that thou art he that was promised unto Abraham, that should come, bless us, and deliver us. Howbeit, Peter yet wist[1] not, by what means. But now it is opened throughout all the world, that, through the offering of his body and the blood, that offering is a satisfaction for the sin of all that repent, and a purchasing of whatsoever they can ask, to keep them in favour; and that they sin no more. And Christ answered, 'Upon this rock I will build my congregation': that is, upon this faith. And against the rock of this faith can no sin, no hell, no devil, no lies, nor error prevail.

[1] Knew.

For whatsoever any man hath committed, if he repent and come to this rock, he is safe. And that this faith is the only way by which the church of Christ goeth unto God, and unto the inheritance of all his riches, testify all the apostles and prophets, and all the scripture, with signs and miracles, and all the blood of martyrs. And whosoever goeth unto God, and unto forgiveness of sins, or salvation, by any other way than this, the same is an heretic out of the right way, and not of Christ's church.

For this knowledge maketh a man of the church. And the church is Christ's body (Col. 1); and every person of the church is a member of Christ (Eph. 5). Now it is no member of Christ that hath not Christ's Spirit in it (Rom. 8); as it is no part of me, or member of my body, wherein my soul is not present and quickeneth it. And then, if a man be none of Christ's, he is not of his church.

How a true member of Christ's church sinneth not; and how he is yet a sinner

Furthermore, he that hath this faith cannot sin, and therefore cannot be deceived with damnable errors. For by this faith we be (as I said) born of God. Now 'he that is born of God cannot sin, for his seed dwelleth in him, and he cannot therefore sin, because he is born of God' (1 John 3); which seed is the Holy Ghost, that keepeth a man's heart from consenting unto sin. And therefore it is a false conclusion that M. More holdeth, how that a man may have a right faith joined with all kinds of abomination and sin.

And yet every member of Christ's congregation is a sinner, and sinneth daily; some more and some less. For it is written, (1 John 1) 'If we say we have no sin, we deceive ourselves, and the truth is not in us.' And again, 'If we say we have not sinned, we make him a liar, and his word is not in us.' And Paul (Rom. 7) saith, 'That good which I would, that do I not; but that evil which I would not, that do I. So it is not I that do it (saith he), but sin that dwelleth in me.' Thus are we sinners, and no sinners: no sinners, if thou look unto the profession of our hearts toward the law of God; on our repentance and sorrow that we have, both because we have sinned, and also because we be yet full of sin still; and unto the promises of mercy in our Saviour Christ; and unto our faith. Sinners are we, if thou look unto the frailty of our flesh; which is as the weakness of one that is newly recovered out of a great disease, by the reason whereof our deeds are imperfect; and by the reason whereof also, when occasions be great, we fall into horrible deeds, and the fruit of the sin which remaineth in our members breaketh out. Notwithstanding yet the Spirit leaveth us not, but rebuketh us, and bringeth us home again unto our profession: so that we never cast off the yoke of God from our necks, neither yield up ourselves unto sin for to serve it, but fight afresh, and begin a new battle.

How a Christian man cannot err, and how he may yet err

And as they sin not, so they err not. And on the other side as they sin, so they err: but never unto death and damnation. For they never sin of purpose, nor hold any error maliciously, sinning against the Holy Ghost; but of weakness and infirmity: as good obedient children, though they love their father's commandments, yet break them oft by the reason of their weakness. And as they cannot yield themselves bond unto sin, to serve it, even so they cannot err in any thing that should be against the promises which are in Christ. And in other things their errors be not unto damnation, though they be never so great, because they hold them not maliciously: as now, if some, when they read in the New Testament of Christ's brethren, would think that they were our lady's children, after the birth of Christ (because they know not the use of speaking of the scripture or of the Hebrews, how that nigh kinsmen be called brethren, or haply they might be Joseph's children by some first wife), neither can have any to teach them for tyranny that is so great; yet could it not hurt them, though they died therein, because it hurteth not that redemption that is in Christ's blood: for though she had none but Christ, I am therefore never the more saved; neither yet the less, though she had had. And in such like an hundred, that pluck not a man's faith from Christ, they might err, and yet be nevertheless saved; no, though the contrary were written in the gospel. For as in other sins, as soon as they be rebuked, they repent; even so here, as soon as they were better taught, they should immediately knowledge their error, and not resist.

But they which maliciously maintain opinions against the scripture, or that they cannot be proved by the scripture; or such as make no matter unto the scripture and salvation that is in Christ, whether they be true or no; and for the blind zeal of them make sects, breaking the unity of Christ's church, for whose sake they ought to suffer all things; and rise against their neighbours, whom they ought to love as themselves, to slay them; such men, I say, are fallen from Christ, and make an idol of their opinions. For except they put trust in such opinions, and thought them necessary unto salvation, or with a cankered conscience went about to deceive for some filthy purpose; they would never break the unity of faith, or yet slay their brethren. Now is this a plain conclusion, that both they that trust in their own works, and they also that put confidence in their own opinions, be fallen from Christ, and err from the way of faith that is in Christ's blood, and therefore are none of Christ's church, because they be not built upon the rock of faith.

Faith is ever assailed and fought withal

Moreover, this our faith which we have in Christ is ever fought against, ever assailed and beaten at with desperation: not when we sin only, but also in all temptations of adversity, into which God bringeth us to nurture us, and to shew us our own hearts, the hypocrisy and false thoughts that there lie hid, our almost no faith at all, and as little love, even then haply when we thought ourselves most perfect of all. For when temptations come, we cannot stand; when we have sinned, faith is feeble; when wrong is done us, we cannot forgive;

in sickness, in loss of goods, and in all tribulations, we be impatient; when our neighbour needeth our help, that we must depart[1] with him of ours, then love is cold.

And thus we learn and feel that there is no goodness nor yet power to do good, but of God only. And in all such temptations our faith perisheth not utterly, neither our love and consent unto the law of God; but they be weak, sick, and wounded, and not clean dead: as a good child, whom the father and mother have taught nurture and wisdom, loveth his father and all his commandments, and perceiveth of the goodness shewed him, that his father loveth him, and that all his father's precepts are unto his wealth and profit, and that his father commandeth him nothing for any need that his father hath thereof, but seeketh his profit only, and therefore hath a good faith unto all his father's promises, and loveth all his commandments, and doth them with good will, and with good will goeth to school; and by the way haply he seeth company play, and with the sight is taken and ravished of his memory, and forgetteth himself, and standeth and beholdeth, and falleth to play also, forgetting father and mother, all their kindness, all their laws, and his own profit thereto: howbeit, the knowledge of his father's kindness, the faith of his promises, and the love that he hath again unto his father, and the obedient mind, are not utterly quenched, but lie hid, as all things do when a man sleepeth or lieth in a trance. And as soon as he hath played out all his lusts, or

[1] Depart: part, divide.

been warned in the mean season, he cometh again unto his old profession. Neverthelater, many temptations go over his heart, and the law, as a right hang-man, tormenteth his conscience, and goeth nigh to persuade him that his father will cast him away and hang him, if he catch him; so that he is like, a great while, to run away, rather than to return unto his father again. Fear and dread of rebuke, and of loss of his father's love, and of punishment, wrestle with the trust which he hath in his father's goodness, and as it were give his faith a fall. But it riseth again as soon as the rage of the first brunt is past, and his mind more quiet. And the goodness of his father and his old kindness cometh unto remembrance, either of his own affections, or by the comfort of some other. And he believeth that his father will not cast him away, or destroy him, and hopeth that he will no more do so. And upon that he getteth him home, dismayed, but not altogether faithless. The old kindnesses will not let him despair. Howbeit, all the world cannot set his heart at rest, until the pain be past, and until he have heard the voice of his father, that all is forgiven.

The manner and order of our election

Even so goeth it with God's elect. God chooseth them first, and they not God; as thou readest, John 15. And then he sendeth forth and calleth them, and sheweth them his good will, which he beareth unto them, and maketh them see both their own damnation in the law, and also the mercy that is laid up for them in Christ's blood, and thereto what he will have them do. And then, when we see his mercy, we love him again, and choose him, and submit ourselves unto his laws, to walk in them. For when we err not in wit, reason, and judgment of things, we cannot err in will and choice of things. The choice of a man's will doth naturally, and of her own accord, follow the judgment of a man's reason, whether he judge right or wrong: so that in teaching only resteth the pith of a man's living. Howbeit, there be swine that receive no learning but to defile it; and there be dogs, that rent all good learning with their teeth. And there be pope-holy, which, following a righteousness of their own feigning, resist the righteousness of God in Christ. And there be that cannot attend to hearken unto the truth, for rage of lusts, which, when lusts abate, come and obey well enough.

And therefore a Christian man must be patient and suffer long, to win his brother to Christ, that he which attendeth not today, may receive grace and hear tomorrow. We see some at their very latter end, when cold fear of death hath quenched the heat of their appetites, learn and consent unto the truth; whereunto before they could give none care, for the wild rages of lusts that blinded their wits.

And though God's elect cannot so fall that they rise not again, because that the mercy of God ever waiteth upon them, to deliver them from evil, as the care of a kind father waiteth upon his son, to warn him and to keep him from occasions, and to call him back again if he be gone too far; yet they forget themselves oft-times, and sink down into trances, and fall asleep in lusts for a season: but as soon as they be awaked, they repent, and come again without resistance. God now and then withdraweth his hand and leaveth them unto their own strength, to make them feel that there is no power to do good but of God only, lest they should be proud of that which is none of theirs. God laid so sore a weight of persecution upon David's back, that passed his strength to bear; so that he cried oft out of his psalms, saying, that he had lived well, and followed the right way of God in vain: for the more he kept himself from sin, the worse it went with him, as he thought; and the better with his enemy Saul, the worse he was. Yet God left him not there, but comforted him; and shewed him things which before he wist not of, how that the saints must be patient, and abide God's harvest, until the wickedness of ungodly sinners be full ripe, that God may reap it in due season.

God also suffered occasions, stronger than David, to fall upon him, and to carry him clean out of the way. Was he not ready for a churlish answer to have slain Nabal, and all the males of his house, so much as the child in the cradle? Howbeit, God withheld him and kept him back from that evil through the wisdom of Abigail. How long slumbered he, or rather how hard in sleep was he, in the adultery of Bathsheba, and in the murder of her husband Uriah! But at both times, as soon as he was rebuked, and his fault told him, he repented immediately, and turned again meekly. Now in all that long time, from the adultery of Bathsheba, until the prophet Nathan rebuked him, he had not lost his faith, nor yet his love unto the laws of God, no more than a man loseth his wits when he is asleep: he had forgot himself only, and had not maliciously cast off the yoke of God's commandments from off his neck. There is no man so good, but that there cometh a time upon him, when he feeleth in himself no more faith, or love unto God, than a sick man oft-times feeleth the taste of his meat which he eateth.

And in like manner the apostles of Christ at his passion were astonished and amazed, and in such a storm of temptations, for the sudden change from so great glory into so vile and shameful death, that they had forgot all the miracles, and all the words which he had told them before, how that he should be betrayed and delivered on the same manner unto death. Moreover, they never understood that saying of his death, because their hearts were alway heavy, and overladen with earthly thoughts. For though they saw him raise up other, yet who should raise him up, when he were dead, they could not comprehend. Read what thou read canst, and thou shalt find no temptation like unto that from the creation of the world, or so great as it, by the hundred part: so that the wonderful sudden change and the terrible sight of his passion, and of his most cruel and most vile death; and the loss of whom they so greatly loved, that their hearts would fain have died with him; and the fear of their own death; and the impossibility that a man should rise again of his own power; so occupied their minds, and so astonished them and amazed them, that they could receive no comfort, either of the scripture, or of the miracles which they had seen Christ do; nor of the monitions and warnings wherewith he had warned them before; neither of the women that brought them tidings that he was risen. The sword of temptations, with fear, sorrow, mourning, and weeping, had deeply pierced their hearts, and the cruel sight had so cumbered their minds, that they could not believe death put off and overcome, until Christ himself came: yea, and when they first saw him, they were astonished for wondering and joy together, that thoughts arose in their hearts, 'Alas, is this he, or doth some spirit mock us?' He was fain to let them feel him, and to eat with them, to strength their faiths.

Howbeit there was none of them that was fallen in his heart from Christ. For as soon as the women brought word, Peter and John ran into the sepulchre, and saw, and wondered, and would fain have believed that he was risen; and longed for him, but could not believe; the wound of temptation being greater than that it could be healed with the preaching of a woman, without any other miracle. Joseph of Arimathea and Nicodemus, which, while he yet lived, durst not be aknowen of[1] him, as soon as he was dead begged his body, and buried him boldly. And the women, as soon as it was lawful to work, prepared their anointments with all diligence. And the hearts of the disciples, that went to Emmaus, burned in their breasts to hear him spoken of. And Thomas had not forsaken Christ, but could not believe until he saw him; and yet desired and

[1] Acknowledge.

66

longed to see him, and rejoiced when he saw him, and for joy cried out, 'My Lord, my God!' There was none of them that ever railed on him, and came so far forth to say, 'He was a deceiver, and wrought with the devil's craft all this while, and see whereto he is come in the end: we defy[1] him and all his works, false wretch that he was, and his false doctrine also.' And thereto must they have come at the last, when fear, sorrow, and wondering had been past, if they had not been prevented and holp in the mean time.

Yea, and Peter, as soon as he had denied Christ, came to himself immediately, and went out and wept bitterly for sorrow. And thus ye see that Peter's faith failed not, though it were oppressed for a time: so that we need to seek no glosses for the text that Christ said to Peter, how that his faith should not fail.

'Yes, saith M. More, it failed in himself, but was reserved in our lady.'[2] But let us see the text and their gloss together.

---

[1] Used as in old French, for distrust.

[2] 'Upon Peter's first confession of the right faith, that Christ was God's Son, our Lord made him his universal vicar, and under him head of his church; and that for his successor he should be the first upon whom, and whose firm confessed faith, he would build his church, and of any that was only man make him the first, and chief head and ruler thereof. Therefore he shewed him that his faith, i.e. to wete [know] the faith by him confessed, should never fail in his church; nor never did it, notwithstanding his denying. For yet stood still the light of faith in our lady; of whom we read in the gospel, continual assistance to her sweetest son, without fleeing or flitting. And in all other we find either fleeing from him, one time or other, or else doubt of his resurrection after his death, his dear mother only except. For the signification and remembrance whereof the church yearly, in the *Tenebræ* lessons, leaveth her candle burning still, when all the remnant, that signifieth his apostles, be one by one put out. And sith [since] his faith that he professed abode in our lady, the promise that God made was, as it seemeth, meant to him but as head of the church.' More's Dial., ch. xviii. fol. 143. col. 2.

Christ saith, 'Simon, Simon, Satan seeketh you, to sift you as men sift wheat; but I have prayed for thee that thy faith shall not fail: wherefore when thou art come unto thyself again, strength thy brethren.' Now put this wise gloss thereto; and see how they agree together! 'Simon, Satan seeketh to sift you as wheat, but I have prayed for thee, that my mother's faith shall not fail: wherefore when thou art come to thyself again, according as my prayer hath obtained for thee that my mother's faith shall not fail, strength thy brethren.' Now say ye, is not this a proper text, and well framed together? Do ye not think there is as much wit in the head of mad Colins,[1] as in the brains of such expositors?

Whether the pope and his sect be Christ's church or no

That the pope and his spirits be not the church, may this wise be proved. He that hath no faith to be saved through Christ, is not of Christ's church. The pope believeth not to be saved through Christ: for he teacheth to trust in holy works for the remission of sins and salvation; as in the works of penance, enjoined in vows; in pilgrimage; in chastity; in other men's prayers and holy living; in friars and friars' coats; in saints' merits; and, the significations put out, he teacheth to believe in the deeds of the ceremonies and of the sacrament, ordained

---

[1] The unhappy gentleman whose derangement was thus a matter of notoriety, was burnt for a heretic, about ten years after this mention of him, to revenge some insult against the reigning superstition, which he had perpetrated with a madman's heedlessness of the consequences. An account of the origin of his calamity, and of the offence for which some said that he was so cruelly treated, may be seen in Foxe's *Acts and Mon.* B. viii.

at the beginning to preach unto us, and to do us service, and not that we should believe in them and serve them. And a thousand such superstitiousnesses setteth he before us, instead of Christ to believe in; neither Christ nor God's word, neither honourable to God nor serviceable unto our neighbour, nor profitable unto ourselves for the taming of the flesh; which all are the denying of Christ's blood.

Another reason is this. Whosoever believeth in Christ, consenteth that God's law is good. The pope consenteth not that God's law is good. For he hath forbidden lawful wedlock unto all his,[1] over whom he reigneth as a temporal tyrant with laws of his own making, and not as a brother exhorting them to keep Christ's; and he hath granted unlawful whoredom unto as many as bring money; as through Dutchland every priest, paying a gildren unto the archdeacon, shall freely and quietly have his whore, and put her away at his pleasure, and take another at his own lust;[2] as they do in Wales, in Ireland, Scotland, France, and Spain.[3] And in England, thereto, they be not few which have licences to keep whores, some of the pope, and some of their ordinaries; and when the parishens go to law with them, to put away their whores, the bishop's

[1] That is, to the whole body of ecclesiastics, and members of every monastic order.

[2] By Dutchland, Tyndale means Germany; and that licensing of sin, to which he alludes, had formed the ninety-first article in the list of a hundred grievances transmitted to pope Adrian IV from the diet of Nuremberg, not more than eight years before Tyndale's composing this answer. These 'Centum gravamina nationis Germanicæ' were published in 4to. at Nuremberg, 1523.

[3] In one of those national ecclesiastical councils held at Toledo, by which Spain was in a manner governed at that period, canon xvii.

officers mock them, poll them, and make them spend their thrifts, and the priests keep their whores still. Howbeit, in very deed, since they were rebuked by the preaching of Wycliffe, our English spiritualty have laid their snares unto men's wives, to cover their abominations, though they bide not alway secret.

Thereto all Christian men, if they have done amiss, repent when their faults be told them. The spiritualty repent not; but, of very lust and consent to sin, persecute both the scripture wherewith they be rebuked, and also them that warn them to amend, and make heretics of them and burn them. And besides that, the pope hath made a plain decree, in which he commandeth, saying, 'Though the pope sin never so grievously, and draw with him to hell by his ensample thousands innumerable, yet let no man be so hardy to rebuke him. For he is head over all; and none over him.' *Distinct.* xl. *Si Papa.*

And Paul saith, (Rom. 13) 'Let every soul obey the higher powers', that are ordained to punish sin. The pope will not, nor let any of his.

And Paul chargeth (1 Cor. 5.): 'If he that is a brother be an whore-keeper, a drunkard, covetous, an extortioner, or a railer', and so forth, that we 'have no fellowship with him; no, not so much as to eat in his company'. But the pope with violence compelleth us to have such in honour, to receive the sacraments of them, to hear their masses, and to believe all they say; and yet they will not let us see whether they say truth or no. And he compelleth ten parishes to pay their tithes and offerings unto one such, to go and run at riot at their cost, and to do nought therefor. And a thousand such like doth the pope, contrary unto Christ's doctrine.

The arguments wherewith the pope would prove himself the church are solved

Notwithstanding because, as they be all shaven, they be all shameless to affirm that they be the right church and cannot err, though all the world seeth that not one of them is in the right way, and that they have with utter defiance forsaken both the doctrine and living of Christ and of all his apostles; let us see the sophistry wherewith they would persuade it. One of their high reasons is this: The church, say they, was before the heretics; and the heretics came ever out of the church, and left it. And they were before all them which they now call heretics and Lutherans, and the Lutherans came out of them, etc. Wherefore they be the right church, and the other heretics indeed, as they be called.[1] Well, I will likewise dispute. First, the right church was under Moses and Aaron, and so forth; in whose rooms sat the scribes and Pharisees and high priests in the time of Christ. And they were before Christ. And Christ and his apostles came out of them, and departed from them, and left them. Wherefore the scribes, Pharisees, and high priests were the right church; and Christ, and his apostles and disciples, heretics, and a damnable sect! And so the Jews are yet in the right way, and we in error. And

[1] The heading of ch. II. B. II. of More's Dial. is, 'The author sheweth that no sect of such as the church taketh for heretics can be the church; forasmuch as the church was before all them, as the tree from which all those withered branches be fallen.'

of truth, if their blind reason be good, then is this argument so too: for they be like, and are both one thing.

But inasmuch as 'the kingdom of God standeth not in words', as Paul saith, 'but in power'; therefore look unto the marrow and pith of the thing's self, and let vain words pass. Under Abraham, Isaac, and Jacob was the church great in faith, and small in number. And as it increased in number, so it decreased in faith, until the time of Moses. And out of those unbelievers God stirred up Moses, and brought them unto the faith right again. And Moses left a glorious church, both in faith and the cleaving unto the word of God; and delivered them unto Joshua, Eleazar, Phineas, and Caleb.

But as soon as the generation of them that saw the miracles of God were dead, they fell to idolatry immediately; as thou seest in the Bible. And God, when he had delivered them into captivity for to chastise their wickedness, stirred them up a prophet evermore, to call them unto his testament again. And so he did well nigh an hundred times, I suppose, ere Christ came; for they never bode any space in the right faith. And against the coming of Christ, the scribes, Pharisees, Caiaphas, Annas, and the elders, were crept up into the seat of Moses, Aaron, and the holy prophets and patriarchs, and succeeded them lineally, and had the scripture of God; but even in captivity, to make merchandise of it, and to abuse it unto their own glory and profit. And though they kept the people from outward idolatry of worshipping of images with the heathen, yet they brought them into a worse inward idolatry, of a false faith and trust in their own deeds, and in vain traditions of their own feigning; and had put out the significations of all the ceremonies and sacraments of the old Testament; and taught the people to believe in the work's self, and had corrupted the scripture with false glosses: as thou mayest see in the gospel, how Christ warneth his disciples to beware of the leaven of the Pharisees, which was their false doctrine and glosses. And in another place he rebuked the scribes and the Pharisees, saying: 'Wo be to them,' because they had taken away the key of knowledge, and had shut up the kingdom of heaven, and neither would enter in themselves nor suffer them that would. How had they shut it up? Verily with their traditions and false glosses; which they had sewed to the scripture in plain places; and in the taking away the meaning of the ceremonies and sacrifices, and teaching to believe in the work.

And our hypocrites are in like manner crept up into the seat of Christ and of his apostles, by succession; not to do the deeds of Christ and his apostles, but for lucre only (as the nature of the wily fox is, to get him an hole made with another beast's labour), and to make merchandise of the people with feigned words, as Peter warned us before [2 Pet. 2]; and to do according as Christ and all his apostles prophesied, how they should beguile, and lead out of the right way, all them that had no love to follow and live after the truth.

And in like manner have they corrupt the scripture, and blinded the right way with their own constitutions, with traditions of dumb ceremonies; with taking away the significations of the sacraments, to make us believe in the work of the sacraments first, whereby they might the better make us believe in works of their setting up afterward; and with false glosses which they have patched to the scripture in plain places, to destroy the literal sense, for to set up a false feigned sense of allegories, when there is none such. And thereby they have stopt up the gates of heaven, the true knowledge of Christ, and have made their own bellies the door. For through their bellies must thou creep, and there leave all that fall behind thee.

And such blind reasons as ours make against us, made they against Christ, saying, Abraham is our father; we be Moses' disciples: how knoweth he the understanding of the scripture, seeing he never learned of any of us? Only the cursed, unlearned people, that know not the scripture, believe in him. Look whether any of the rulers or Pharisees do believe in him! [John 7; 8.]

Wherefore, the scripture truly understood, after the plain places and general articles of the faith, which thou findest in the scripture, and the ensamples that are gone before, will alway testify who is the right church. Though the Pharisees succeeded the patriarchs and prophets, and had the scripture of them; yet they were heretics, and fallen from the faith of them and from their living. And Christ and his disciples, and John the Baptist, departed from the Pharisees, which were heretics, unto the right sense of the scripture, and unto the faith and living of the patriarchs and prophets, and rebuked the Pharisees: as thou seest how Christ calleth them hypocrites, dissimulers, blind guides, and painted sepulchres. And John called them the generation of vipers and serpents. Of John the angel said unto his father, 'He shall turn many of the children of Israel unto their Lord God'; which yet, before John, believed after a fleshly understanding in God, and thought themselves in the right way. And, 'He shall turn the hearts of the fathers unto the children': that is, he shall, with his preaching and true interpreting of the scripture, make such a spiritual heart in the children, as was in their fathers, Abraham, Isaac, and Jacob. And, 'He shall turn the disobedient unto the obedience of the righteous, and prepare the Lord a perfect people': that is, them that had set up a righteousness of their own, and were therefore disobedient unto the righteousness of faith, shall he convert from their blindness unto the wisdom of them that believed in God, to be made righteous; and with those fathers shall he give the children eagles' eyes, to spy out Christ and his righteousness, and to forsake their own, and so to become perfect.

And after the same manner, though our popish hypocrites succeed Christ and his apostles, and have their scripture, yet they be fallen from the faith and living of them, and are heretics, and had need of a John Baptist to convert them. And we depart from them unto the true scripture, and unto the faith and living thereof, and rebuke them in like manner. And as they which depart from the faith of the true church are heretics, even so they that depart from the church of heretics and false feigned faith of hypocrites, are the true church; which thou shalt alway know by their faith, examined by the scripture, and by their profession and consent to live according unto the laws of God.

Another argument

Another like blind reason they have, wherein is all their trust. As we come out of them and they not of us, so we receive the scripture of them, and they not of us. How know we that it is the scripture of God, and true, but because they teach us so? How can we believe, except we first believe that they be the church, and cannot err in any thing that pertaineth unto our soul's health? For if a man tell me of a marvellous thing, whereof I can have no other knowledge than by his mouth only; how should I give credence, except I believe that the man were so honest that he could not lie, or would not lie? Wherefore, we must believe that they be the right church that cannot err, or else we can believe nought at all.[1]

This wise reason is their shot anchor, and all their hold, their refuge to fly unto, and chief stone in their foundation; whereon they have built all their lies, and all their mischief that they have wrought this eight hundred years. And this

[1] 'Finally, to put out of question which is Christ's very church, sith it is agreed between us, and granted through Christendom, and a conclusion very true, that by the church we know the scripture, which church is that by which we know the scripture? Is it not this company and congregation of all these nations, that without factions taken, and precision from the remnant, profess the name and faith of Christ? By this church know we the scripture, and this is the very church; and this hath begun at Christ, and hath had him for their head, and St Peter his vicar after him, the head under him, and alway since the successors of him continually.'—More's Dialogue, B. II. ch. v. p. 185. col. 2.

reason do the Jews lay unto our charge this day; and this reason doth chiefly blind them, and hold them still in obstinacy. Our spirits first falsify the scripture to stablish their lies; and when the scripture cometh to light, and is restored unto the true understanding, and their juggling spied, and they like to suffer shipwreck, then they cast out this anchor: They be the church and cannot err; their authority is greater than the scripture; and the scripture is not true, but because they say so and admit it. And therefore, whatsoever they affirm, is of as great authority as the scripture.

Notwithstanding, as I said, the kingdom of heaven standeth not in words of man's wisdom, but in power and spirit. And therefore look unto the examples of the scripture, and so shalt thou understand. And of an hundred examples between Moses and Christ, where the Israelites fell from God, and were ever restored by one prophet or other, let us take one, even John the Baptist. John went before Christ to prepare his way, that is, to bring men unto the knowledge of their sins, and unto repentance, through true expounding of the law, which is the only way unto Christ: for except a man knowledge his sins, and repent of them, he can have no part in Christ. Of John Christ saith (Matt. 17), that 'he was Elijah that should come, and restore all things': that is, he should restore the scripture unto the right sense again; which the Pharisees had corrupted with the leaven of their false glosses, and vain fleshly traditions. He made crooked things straight, as it is written, and rough smooth. Which is also to be understood of the scripture, which the Pharisees had made crooked, wresting them unto a false sense with wicked glosses; and so rough that no man could walk in the way of them. For when God said, 'Honour father and mother,' meaning, that we should obey them, and also help them at their need, the Pharisees put this gloss thereto, out of their own leaven, saying: 'God is thy father and mother. Wherefore, whatsoever need thy father and mother have, if thou offer to God, thou art held excused. For it is better to offer to God, than to thy father and mother; and so much more meritorious, as God is greater than they: yea, and God hath done more for thee than they, and is more thy father and mother than they.' As ours now affirm, 'That it is more meritorious to offer to God and his holy dead saints, than unto the poor living saints.' And when God had promised the people a Saviour, to come and bless them, and save them from their sins; the Pharisees taught to believe in holy works to be saved by, as if they offered and gave to be prayed for: as ours, as oft as we have a promise to be forgiven at the repentance of the heart through Christ's blood-shedding, put to, 'Thou must first shrive[1] thyself to us of every syllable, and we must lay our hands on thine head, and whistle out thy sins, and enjoin thee penance to make satisfaction. And yet art thou but loosed from the sin only that thou shalt not come into hell; but thou must yet suffer for every sin seven years in purgatory, which is as hot as hell, except thou buy it out of the pope.' And if thou ask, 'By what means the pope giveth such pardon?' they answer, 'Out of

[1] Confess.

the merits of Christ.' And thus at the last they grant, against themselves, that Christ hath not only deserved for us the remission of our sins, but also the forgiveness of that gross and fleshly imagined purgatory, save thou must buy it out of the pope. And with such traditions they took away the key of knowledge, and stopped up the kingdom of heaven, that no man could enter in.

And as I said, they taught the people to believe in the deeds of the ceremonies, which God ordained, not to justify, but to be signs of promises, by which they that believed were justified. But the Pharisees put out the significations, and quenched the faith, and taught to be justified by the work, as ours have served us.

For our sacraments were once but signs; partly of what we should believe, to stir us up unto faith; and partly what we should do, to stir us up to do the law of God; and were not works to justify.

Now make this reason unto John, and unto many prophets that went before him and did as he did; yea, and unto Christ himself and his apostles; and thou shalt find them all heretics, and the scribes and Pharisees good men, if that reason be good. Therefore, this-wise thou mayest answer. No thanks unto the heads of the church, that the scripture was kept, but unto the mercy of God. For as they had destroyed the right sense of it, for their lucre sake, even so would they have destroyed it also, if they could, rather than the people should have come unto the right understanding of it; as they slew the true interpreters and preachers of it. And even so, no thanks unto our hypocrites, that the scripture is kept, but unto the bottomless mercy of God.

For as they have destroyed the right sense of it with their leaven; and as they destroy daily the true preachers of it; and as they keep it from the lay-people, that they should not see how they juggle with it; even so would they destroy it also, could they bring it about, rather than we should come by the true understanding of it, were it not that God provided otherwise for us. For they have put the stories, that should in many things help us, clean out of the way, as nigh as they could. They have corrupt the legend and lives almost of all saints. They have feigned false books, and put them forth; some in the name of St Jerome, some in the name of St Augustine, in the name of St Cyprian, St Dionyse, and other holy men; which are proved none of theirs, partly by the style and Latin, and partly by authentic stories. And as the Jews have set up a book of traditions called Talmud, to destroy the sense of the scripture; unto which they give faith, and unto the scripture none at all, be it never so plain, but say it cannot be understood, save by the Talmud: even so have ours set up their Duns, their Thomas, and a thousand like draff, to stablish their lies through falsifying the scripture; and say that it cannot be understood without them, be it never so plain. And if a man allege an holy doctor against them, they gloss him out as they do the scripture; or will not hear; or say the church hath otherwise determined.

Now therefore, when they ask us how we know it is the scripture of God; ask them how John Baptist knew, and other prophets, which God stirred up in all such times as the scripture was in like captivity under hypocrites? Did John believe that the scribes, Pharisees, and high priests, were the true church of God, and had his Spirit, and could not err? Who taught the eagles to spy out their prey? Even so the children of God spy out their Father; and Christ's elect spy out their Lord, and trace out the paths of his feet, and follow; yea, though he go upon the plain and liquid water, which will receive no step, and yet there they find out his foot: his elect know him, but the world knoweth him not (John 1). If the world know him not, and thou call the world pride, wrath, envy, covetousness, sloth, gluttony, and lechery, then our spiritualty know him not. Christ's sheep hear the voice of Christ (John 10); where the world of hypocrites, as they know him not, even so the wolves hear not his voice, but compel the scripture to hear them, and to speak what they lust.

And therefore, except the Lord of Sabaoth had left us seed, we had been all as Sodom and Gomorrah, said Isaiah in his first chapter. And even so said Paul in his time [Rom. 11]. And even so say we in our time, that the Lord of the hosts hath saved him seed, and hath gathered him a flock, to whom he hath given ears to hear that the hypocritish wolves cannot hear, and eyes to see that the blind leaders of the blind cannot see, and an heart to understand that the generation of poisoned vipers can neither understand nor know.

If they allege St Augustine, which saith, 'I had not believed the gospel, except the authority of the church had moved me': I answer, as they abuse that saying of the holy man, even so they allege all the scripture, and all that they bring for them, even in a false sense. St Augustine, before he was converted, was an heathen man, and a philosopher, full of worldly wisdom, unto whom the preaching of Christ is but foolishness, saith Paul (1 Cor. 1). And he disputed with blind reasons of worldly wisdom against the Christians. Nevertheless, the earnest living of the Christians, according unto their doctrine, and the constant suffering of persecution and adversity for their doctrine's sake, moved him, and stirred him to believe that it was no vain doctrine; but that it must needs be of God, in that it had such power with it. For it happeneth that they which will not hear the word at the beginning, are afterward moved by the holy conversation of them that believe: as Peter warneth Christian wives that had heathen husbands, that would not hear the truth preached, to live so godly that they might win their heathen husbands with holy conversation. And Paul saith, 'How knowest thou, Christian wife, whether thou shalt win thine heathen husband?' With holy conversation, meant he: for many are won with godly living, which at the first either will not hear, or cannot believe. And that is the authority that St Augustine meant. But if we shall not believe till the living of the spiritualty convert us, we be like to bide long enough in unbelief.

And when they ask, whether we received the scripture of them? I answer, 'That they which come after receive the scripture of them that go before.' And when they ask, 'Whether we believe not that it is God's word, by the reason that they tell us so?' I answer, 'That there are two manner faiths, an historical faith, and a feeling faith.' The historical faith hangeth of the truth and honesty of the teller, or of the common fame and consent of many: as if one told me that the Turk had won a city, and I believed it, moved with the honesty of the man; now if there come another that seemeth more honest, or that hath better persuasions that it is not so, I think immediately that he lied, and lose my faith again. And a feeling faith is as if a man were there present when it was won, and there were wounded, and had there lost all that he had, and were taken prisoner there also: that man should so believe, that all the world could not turn him from his faith. Then, even likewise, if my mother had blown on her finger, and told me that the fire would burn me, I should have believed her with an historical faith, as we believe the stories of the world, because I thought she would not have mocked me. And so I should have done, if she had told me that the fire had been cold, and would not have burned; but as soon as I had put my finger in the fire, I should have believed, not by the reason of her, but with a feeling faith, so that she could not have persuaded me afterward the contrary. So now with an historical faith I may believe that the scripture is God's, by the teaching of them; and so I should have done, though they had told me that Robin Hood had been the scripture of God: which faith is but an opinion, and therefore abideth ever fruitless; and falleth away, if a more glorious reason be made unto me, or if the preacher live contrary.

But of a feeling faith it is written (John 6), 'They shall be all taught of God.' That is, God shall write it in their hearts with his Holy Spirit. And Paul also testifieth (Rom. 8), 'The Spirit beareth record unto our spirit, that we be the sons of God.' And this faith is none opinion; but a sure feeling, and therefore ever fruitful. Neither hangeth it of the honesty of the preacher, but of the power of God, and of the Spirit: and, therefore, if all the preachers of the world would go about to persuade the contrary, it would not prevail ; no more than though they would make me believe the fire were cold, after that I had put my finger therein. Of this we have an ensample (John 4) of the Samaritanish wife, which left her pitcher, and went into the city, and said, 'Come, and see a man that hath told me all that ever I did. Is not he Christ?' And many of the Samaritans believed, because of the saying of the woman, how that he had told her all that ever she did; and went out unto him, and desired him to come in. Which faith was but an opinion; and no faith that could have lasted, or have brought out fruit. But when they had heard Christ, the Spirit wrought, and made them feel. Whereupon they came unto the woman, and said: 'We believe, not now because of thy saying, but because we have heard ourselves, and know that he is Christ, the Saviour of the world.' For

Christ's preaching was with power and spirit, that maketh a man feel, and know and work too; and not as the scribes and Pharisees preached; and as ours make a man ready to cast his gorge to hear them rave and rage as mad men. And therefore, saith the scripture, 'Cursed is he that trusteth in man, and maketh flesh his arm'; that is to say, his strength. And even so, Cursed is he that hath none other belief, but because men say so. Cursed were he that had none other why to believe than that I so say. And even so cursed is he that believeth only because the pope so saith; and so forth throughout all the men in the world.

EPILOGUE

William Tyndale's Legacy

Robert J. Sheehan

During his life (1494–1536), William Tyndale was greatly hated by the Roman Catholic establishment. Sir Thomas More, the Chancellor of England, described him as 'that beast and hell-hound of the devil's kennel'. King Henry VIII denounced his 'venomous and pestiferous works, erroneous and seditious opinions'. His judicial murder in Vilvorde, Belgium, in October 1536, at the age of 42, was viewed by the Catholic hierarchy as a suitable end for an arch-heretic. There was no end to their hatred for him.

Not everyone was hostile to him, however. Some of the scholars of his day respected his learning. Here was a man who could speak seven languages so fluently that it was impossible to tell from which country he came. Others respected him for his translation work and his theological writings. Tyndale earned the respect of many.

The modern assessment of Tyndale in both evangelical and scholarly circles recognizes that the Roman Catholic fear of him was not misplaced. It has been claimed in the modern world that *William Tyndale was the Reformation in England,* that without his activities the English Reformation would never have occurred.

Even those who would find this assertion an over-statement readily acknowledge Tyndale as *unquestionably the most remarkable figure among the first generation of English Protestants.*

Perhaps one of the most appropriate tributes to the significance of Tyndale is the existence today in Vilvorde, Belgium, the town in which he was executed, of a Protestant Church called the William Tyndale Church of Vilvorde and the William Tyndale Museum which also has been established. He who was so reviled in life is honoured five hundred years later.

Why was William Tyndale so important? How did his work affect the many generations of Christians and others in English society who followed him?

1. Since Tyndale the English people have had the Bible available to them

Years before Tyndale was born, John Wycliffe had produced a translation of the Bible based on the Latin text revered by the Roman Catholic Church. This work was completed about 1382 and revised in 1388. This Bible was produced because Wycliffe believed that every man had the right to read the

Bible for himself. Wycliffe's teachings and Bible were treasured by his disciples, the Lollards, but were totally opposed by the Roman Catholic establishment.

Relentless persecution followed the Lollards throughout the fifteenth century. In 1401 the burning of heretics was legalized. In 1408 a law was passed forbidding any translation of the Bible into English unless authorized by the bishops.

The Lollards clung tenaciously to Wycliffe's translation, although its possession led many to suffering and death, but there was no widespread use of the Bible in English in fifteenth-century England. The Catholic Church in Germany allowed twenty translations of the Bible between 1466 and 1522. The Catholic Church in France permitted two translations of the Bible between 1477 and 1521. The English Church allowed no translations and stigmatized the possession of a Bible in English as an heretical act.

Faced with a church that would not allow the Bible in English and a nation which did not possess a translation made from the Hebrew and Greek, Tyndale vowed to his clerical opponents, 'If God spare my life, ere many years I will cause a boy that driveth the plow shall know more of the Scripture than thou dost.'

Working outside England, first at Cologne and then at Worms, Tyndale had his New Testament translated and, by March 1526, the English New Testament began to flood into England. Each one cost three shillings two pence, a week's wages for a skilled labourer, but demand outstripped supply.

The Roman Catholic King, Church, and clergy did all within their power to suppress Tyndale's New Testament, yet such was the demand for the Bible in English that in September 1538 (eleven years after the first New Testaments arrived) the King and his Government issued a decree that a copy of the Bible in Latin and in English had to be placed by every parson in the choir area of every church *for every man that will to look and read thereon*. The Bible permitted was not Tyndale's Bible in name but the *Coverdale* Bible and the *Matthew* Bible. However, in substance it was Tyndale's work.

Once these Bibles gained circulation in England, the possession of an English Bible by English people was irreversible.

Nor was Tyndale's influence reduced by the passing of time. Ninety per cent of the New Testament of the 1611 King James Version is the translation of William Tyndale.

Under God, the modern English-speaking Christian owes his possession of an English Bible to a man born at the end of the fifteenth century.

2. Tyndale restored the authority of Scripture in the church

In Tyndale's day, the Roman Catholic Church was the ultimate authority. She declared what God had revealed. She had to be obeyed. She determined what true doctrine, true morals, and true ceremonies were.

Modern Catholicism is no different. One of its modern catechisms asks:

How are you to know what God has revealed?
I am to know what God has revealed by the testimony,
teaching and authority of the Catholic Church.

Can the Church err in what she teaches?
The Church cannot err in what she teaches as to faith or
morals, for she is our infallible guide in both.

Tyndale, along with Luther, did not accept that the Church was an infallible teacher. He believed that the Bible was the infallible teacher and that it judged and determined the teaching, morals, and ceremonies of the Church.

When the people had no Bible, they had no way of testing whether the Roman Catholic Church was the true church. When Tyndale gave them the Bible they asked the question and, in their thousands, concluded that the Pope's church was not Christ's church.

In Acts 17:11 the Bereans are commended for testing the teaching of the apostle Paul by comparing it to the Scriptures to see if he was speaking the truth. The Roman Catholic Church had removed this possibility of testing her teachings and claims. Tyndale restored the possibility, and freed us from bondage to the dogmatic assertions of a deceiving church. The English-speaking people owe him an incalculable debt.

3. Tyndale restored the individual's liberty of private interpretation

When the Roman Catholic Church claimed to be the infallible guide to faith and morals, she arrogated to herself the right to be the sole interpreter of Scripture. Her priests alone could say what the Bible meant. Those who had not studied the truth as her priests had should not meddle with it or seek to interpret it. A passive acceptance of the Church's interpretation was required.

The Catholic King Henry VIII was, therefore, horrified to find that the Bible he had been persuaded to have published was a common matter of discussion and dispute among ordinary people. He lamented that the 'most precious jewel, the word of God, is disputed, rhymed, sung and jangled in every alehouse and tavern'. Tyndale's ploughman was reading, discussing, and interpreting the Bible with his friends but without his priest!

Even among young men from Catholic families, the role of the priest was being downgraded. One such, Robert Plumpton, wrote to his mother in 1536, 'As for the understanding of it, doubt not, for God will give knowledge to whom he will give knowledge of the Scriptures, as soon to a shepherd as to a priest, if he ask knowledge of God faithfully.' For young Robert Plumpton, understanding of the Scriptures was a gift of God given to those who sincerely sought it from God. It was not the priest who was needed but the illumination of the Spirit.

Tyndale gave to subsequent generations of Christians the truth that the meaning of Scripture does not come to us through the priest but through the prayerful seeking of God for light upon his word. Tyndale restored the Christian's liberty to study the word of God for himself. Are we using this privilege? Are we approaching God's word with the submissive humility required?

4. Tyndale gave great emphasis to the doctrine of justification by faith alone

Tyndale was not the first man to preach justification by faith alone in England, but by his prologues to the biblical books, his marginal notes to his New Testament, and his written works, he was the chief vehicle for the promotion of this truth in England.

For the Roman Catholic Church, faith was merely an assent to her teachings. This 'faith' was first received by baptism. It had to be constantly restored and renewed by confession and priestly absolution. It had to be accompanied by good works, hope, and love. Faith is just one element in a long list of acts leading to salvation.

For Tyndale, however, there was to be no reliance on faith or good works, hope or love, confession or absolution, or anything else. All our reliance for salvation is on Christ alone. All reliance upon personal merit or activities goes. Our whole trust is in Christ's merits. We are saved by Christ alone or not at all.

Tyndale's connection with Luther in this matter is clear. Tyndale's *Prologue to the Book of Romans* is largely a translation of Luther's comments on this book. Tyndale's commitment to this truth was unwavering. As he sat in prison for one year, one hundred and thirty-five days, awaiting execution, cold and ill, and for the most part in darkness, he took the opportunity of those hours when it was light enough to see, to pen his treatise *Faith alone justifies before God*.

The proclamation of justification by faith alone has resulted in the eternal salvation of innumerable people in England since Tyndale's day. The best tribute the English-speaking people could pay to the memory of William Tyndale would be to trust in the Lord Jesus Christ alone for salvation.

5. Tyndale laid the foundation for the Puritan commitment to godly living

The truth of justification by faith alone, when properly understood, has never been an enemy of godly living. The justified contribute nothing to their salvation but they have a life to live to the praise of God in response to, and as a consequence of, being saved by his grace in Christ.

From 1530 onwards, Tyndale emphasized the twin truths of justification by faith alone and the demonstration of that justification by obedience to God's moral law. This dual emphasis on justification by faith and sanctification by law was to prove foundational and central to Christian thinking in England from the mid-sixteenth century to the end of the seventeenth century. It was to be one of the dominant themes of English Puritanism and it was to become a significant part of the English Reformed tradition.

Tyndale's role in asserting that we are not saved from sin to serve sin, but from sin to obey God, laid the foundation for the Puritan passion for God and godliness. Tyndale established the idea that the justified man is to live his life before man unto the glory of God, and that God is glorified by the justified man's obedience to God's law. In this respect, Tyndale has correctly been called the first of the Puritans.

We, the heirs of Tyndale's legacy, only truly honour him when we share his insistence that *the justified man is to be the godly man, that he who is saved from his disobedience is to demonstrate his salvation by his obedience.*

6. Tyndale established the Puritan approach to interpreting Scripture

In this matter too, Tyndale was the first of the Puritans, or, at least their grandfather! In his doctrinal treatises he set out five significant keys to the interpretation of Scripture that were mediated to the later Puritans through their leader, William Perkins.

- *Firstly, the law has to be interpreted spiritually.* It is not merely concerned with actions but with the motives of the heart. Everything that does not proceed from the heart and is not done out of sincere love is damnable sin. The Puritan concern to reveal the heart and its motives by the convicting preaching of the law is rooted in Tyndale's first emphasis.

- *Secondly, the gospel promises salvation to the repentant as an act of divine mercy and as a consequence of the merits of Christ alone.* So the Puritan emphasis on salvation by grace alone, through faith alone, because of Christ alone, is emphasized in Tyndale. Tyndale referred to the law and the gospel, command and promise as the two keys which open all the Scriptures to us, the two themes above all other themes.

- *Thirdly, Tyndale saw the Bible as full of examples of God's dealings with godly men.* The trials of the godly, their comforts, and their preservation by God were written for our learning.

- *Fourthly, he saw a second type of example, that of the ungodly.* The Scriptures record God's long-suffering towards them, their judicial hardening, and their ultimate destruction. Puritan sermons are particularly notable for their use of biblical illustration. Every principle is clothed in an example, good or bad. Every precept is enforced by an illustration from the historical portions of Scripture. The Puritans practised to the fullest degree what Tyndale preached on this matter.

- *Fifthly, Tyndale agreed with Luther as to the importance of the apostle Paul's Epistle to the Romans.* He described it as 'a light and way unto the whole Scripture'. William Perkins built on this foundation by asserting that a knowledge of Romans and the Gospel of John was the key to the entire Bible.

Several generations of preachers owed their approach to the interpretation of Scripture to Tyndale's guidance. These emphases are just as valid today as then. What amazing insight this man had into Scripture!

7. Tyndale encouraged the idea of individual disobedience to tyrants

It is ironic that Tyndale's most influential book, apart from his New Testament, was *The Obedience of the Christian Man*, published in 1528. In it he argued that subjects, servants, wives, and children should give loyal obedience to their kings, masters, husbands, and parents. He also required priests and popes to be subject to kings. The effect of the book was to place the king over all his subjects and to require them to show him loyal obedience. This book delighted Henry VIII.[1]

However, Tyndale's actions spoke louder than his words. The English bishops would not patronize his translation work. The English clergy were accusing him of heresy. England was not, therefore, a suitable context for his work and so he broke the King's law by leaving England without permission in 1524.

From 1524 until his death in 1536 everything he did, he did as a fugitive from the King's law, being sought by the King's agents. Every book he wrote, even *The Obedience of*

---

[1] David Daniell, in his excellent biography of Tyndale, helpfully discusses this aspect of the reformer's teaching in *The Obedience of the Christian Man*. While clearly subjects are wrong to think of rebellious disobedience, Tyndale also focuses on the relation of the King to his God. 'The ruler is under the religious and moral duty to act in accordance with God's law. He has a heavy and particular burden.' In Daniell's view, 'Tyndale did not offer Henry VIII or anyone else a sovereignty not subject to natural law.' (See *William Tyndale: A Biography* (New Haven & London: Yale University Press, 1994, pb. ed.) p. 242.—*Ed.*

the Christian Man, he wrote illegally. Every one of his books read in England, including his New Testament, was smuggled into the country and read illegally.

Tyndale's actions modified his published teaching. His actions taught that the King was to be obeyed except where he required men to act against their religious convictions. The King's will was the highest human authority, but God's will was a higher authority still.

By his actions, therefore, Tyndale established an authority above that of the King, the authority of God. The Christian man was to allow no one and nothing to hinder his obedience to God. He must do what he believed to be right whatever the consequences.

Tyndale's actions had an immense influence over Protestant thinking and practice. The Tudors and the Stuarts longed to rule as absolute monarchs, their word to be unquestionably obeyed, supreme in both church and state. Tyndale's disobedience began a shift in Protestant thinking. Monarchs could be disobeyed. Rebellion could be legitimate. When the state sets itself to oppose what God commands, we must obey God rather than men.

The momentous events of the Puritan age and the Great Rebellion or English Civil War are rooted in a rejection of Tyndale's *teaching* of total obedience to the state and an acceptance of his *practice* of disobeying the state where the state opposes God. Tyndale's practice is needed again in the modern world. We need to remember that the state has no authority to control our consciences, nor to interfere in our churches, nor to require us to acquiesce in its legalisation of sin. If Tyndale had waited for the permission of the King and the clergy to do his work the English Reformation would never have taken place.

8. Tyndale encouraged the freeing of human thought

During the early Medieval period, known to us as 'The Dark Ages', the Church held an effective control over all areas of human life. Education, science, and art were under her supervision.

During the fifteenth century, however, the Renaissance occurred, bringing with it new approaches in thinking. A great interest developed in going beyond the Medieval period and back to Greece and Rome. Interest grew in Hebrew and Greek language and literature. A whole movement developed devoted to the study of ancient human writings ('humanism').

Renaissance humanists were usually well-educated scholars. They were interested in original sources of information. With regard to the Bible, they wanted to study it in its original languages. Roman Catholic humanists were at the forefront of studying the Hebrew and Greek Bible. For some this led to conversion to Christ and to the 'Protestant' doctrines proclaimed by Martin Luther. For others it led to an opening up of a whole new approach to study where individual scholars could make up their own minds and hold their own opinions without being told what to think by the Church.

At the beginning of the English Reformation, most of the people converted to Christ and liberated to think for themselves were scholars, priests, and university students.

Tyndale's New Testament, however, could be read by, and to, the common people. In 1543 the King was alarmed to find the Bible widely read by the unprivileged classes, *women, artificers, apprentices, journeymen, serving men, husbandmen, and labourers*. He tried to limit its reading to only noblemen, gentlemen, substantial merchants, and gentlewomen. But, of course, it was too late. The ordinary people had been taught by Tyndale's Bible, and God's word was addressed to them. They could read, understand, interpret, and discuss it. They also had minds, opinions, and points of view.

If the common man could have an opinion on religion, why not on education, science, art, politics? Tyndale's Bible gave to the common man a sense of his own right to think for himself. By the time the English Civil War broke out in the next century, many radical, free-thinking groups had arisen and the ordinary man could no longer be treated just as a feudal serf.

The common people heard Jesus gladly. The common people received gladly the New Testament in their own language too. The English people became *the people of the Book* and grew more confident to think their own thoughts without having to be told what to think.

9. Tyndale taught men the dignity of labour

In a class-ridden society where everyone was expected to know his place, the position of the working man in Tudor England was not an enviable one. In some senses he had a little more freedom than the Medieval serf but was less protected from economic factors than the serf had been. The vast majority of the English population lived in grinding poverty as a subservient under-class.

The important people in Tudor England were the kings, the landed gentry, the clergy, and the increasingly significant merchant class. The peasants were merely tools to be used, but without intrinsic value.

Tyndale, along with other Protestant leaders, found within the Scriptures a different view of man. God had made man to work, not to be idle. Each man had his God-given calling, his particular role to fulfil, his God-given work to do. Some were called to rule, others to preach. Some were called to work in the fields, others in the home.

Whatever calling a person had, however significant or insignificant in the eyes of men, as long as that person accepted his calling and sought to fulfil it in a way that would please God, it was work acceptable to God. Tyndale believed that the washing of dishes and the preaching of the word were both legitimate callings, each having their own dignity and their own value in the sight of God.

This view of the dignity of labour, all labour, when properly received from God and done for him, meant that the working man no longer had to view himself as a tool for the use of his superiors but as a servant of God doing the daily round and common task to his glory.

Tyndale's teaching strikes at the pride and the pomposity of the important people. It makes ordinary men and women know that God values them too and calls them to serve him, with the gifts he has given them and in the role he has assigned to them.

10. Tyndale had an enduring effect on English language and literature

No one can deny the immense effect that the King James Version has had on the literature and language of the English-speaking people. Yet most of its New Testament rests on Tyndale's work.

Tyndale has been called a *prophet* of the English language. He seems to have had a unique insight into its structure and knew the exact phrases to coin in order to make it readable and memorable. His English remained standard English for several centuries. His work stood the test of time.

Whatever degree of satisfaction some may feel in modern versions of the Bible, the cry can still be heard, 'If only we had a Tyndale, then we would have a really good modern translation.' That this should be heard five hundred years after his birth is an immense testimony to his unique contribution to the English Reformation, the English Bible, and indeed, the whole course of English history.

William Tyndale was a gift of God to the people of England. The foundations of our Protestant faith, and of our religious, political, and social liberties were laid by him. We would do well to hold firmly to what he gave us, to keep the Holy Bible at the heart of our faith, to trust in Christ alone for salvation, and to maintain our Christian liberties over and against all who would deny them to us. Tyndale's heirs need Tyndale's courage, Tyndale's Bible, and, above all, Tyndale's Saviour.

The Banner of Truth Trust originated in 1957 in London. The founders believed that much of the best literature of historic Christianity had been allowed to fall into oblivion and that, under God, its recovery could well lead not only to a strengthening of the church, but to true revival.

Inter-denominational in vision, this publishing work is now international, and our lists include a number of contemporary authors along with classics from the past. The translation of these books into many languages is encouraged.

A monthly magazine, *The Banner of Truth*, is also published. More information about this and all our publications can be found on our website or supplied by either of the offices below.

THE BANNER OF TRUTH TRUST

3 Murrayfield Road   PO Box 621, Carlisle
Edinburgh, EH12 6EL   Pennsylvania 17013,
UK   USA

www.banneroftruth.org

The Works of William Tyndale

TWO VOLUME SET:

Doctrinal Treatises and Introductions to Different Portions of
the Holy Scriptures

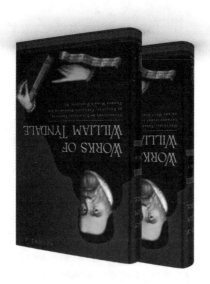

'A reprint of this kind is no mere archaeological curiosity;
one who was so intensely a man of the Bible as Tyndale
was speaks to more ages than his own, and in the following pages we shall find that he has much to say to us, if
we pay heed to what we read.'   — F. F. BRUCE

ISBN 978 1 84871 0 740 | 1,325 pp. | clothbound